Reclaiming Your
JOY

Reclaiming Your
JOY

A Bible Study on Conquering Your Joy-Stealers

LORRAINE HILL

TATE PUBLISHING & Enterprises

Published by Tate Publishing & Enterprises, LLC
127 E. Trade Center Terrace | Mustang, Oklahoma 73064 USA
1.888.361.9473 | www.tatepublishing.com

Tate Publishing is committed to excellence in the publishing industry. The company reflects the philosophy established by the founders, based on Psalm 68:11,
"The Lord gave the word and great was the company of those who published it."

Book design copyright © 2011 by Tate Publishing, LLC. All rights reserved.
Cover design by April Marciszewski
Interior design by Joel Uber

Published in the United States of America

ISBN: 978-1-61346-139-6
1. Religion: Biblical Studies, Bible Study Guides
2. Religion: Christian Life, Inspirational
12.07.18

Dedication

To Shawn, my beloved husband, my greatest gratitude for the endless support and encouragement you have shown me over the years. Thank you for all the humble sacrifices you have made to allow me to become the woman God desires me to be. Your patience, integrity, and faithfulness are a constant support as is your dedication and love for our LORD. I have been blessed beyond measure to have such a godly, loving husband.

And to my children, Noah, Joshua, and Hannah, what a privilege it is to be your mother. How thankful I am that God entrusted your care to me. You bring me such joy. I love you all so very much.

Acknowledgements

This Bible study would never have been possible without the help and assistance of numerous people, many of whom only the LORD knows. So please forgive me if I have missed your name.

Lindy Schuch, words cannot express how much your friendship means to me. My heart rejoices to have such a close friend like you. You have such a passion and love for our LORD. Thank you for encouraging and challenging me. My heartfelt thanks for painstakingly reviewing and evaluating this study with me.

Lanette Sikes, Tricia Owen, Elizabeth Monney, Nicole MacFarlane, Nicole Tarver, Mary Lee Crenshaw, Paula Weatherly, Michelle Lee, Susan Byers, Ashley Bivens - My sweet friends, your dedication to our LORD is humbling and inspiring. I have been uplifted and strengthened by your friendships. Thank you for all your encouragement and help over the years, especially on this study.

Penny Kemp, Peggy Pickens, my great mentors, I am so grateful for the wisdom and faith you have shown me. You are such strong examples of godly women. Thank you for your transparency and for both inspiring and challenging me. You have sharpened me as iron sharpens iron.

Pastor David Lino, Pastor Doug Page, Pastor Craig Reynolds—it has been a great privilege to sit under your teaching. Words can never convey my appreciation for all I have learned from you. My deepest thanks for investing in me and helping me grow in my faith.

Barry Wilson, Lyndsay Witham, Joyce Apel, Chuck Oak, Fred Dallas, Jeff Hiett, Mark Terry, Rose-Ann Dunn, Mary Long, Flo

Avra, Kathyrn Roberts, my humble Second Baptist staff and librarians, many thanks to you. Without your quiet and sacrificial service, this study would never have happened. Thank you for building up and edifying the body of Christ.

The ladies who have done the study, thank you ladies for allowing me to glimpse into your hearts and lives. God has made each of you so beautiful, and I am so grateful that he allowed me to know you.

Tate Publishing, a heartfelt thanks to Tate Publishing for partnering with me in this endeavor. May women everywhere experience the boundless depth and fullness of joy that God offers.

Patrick and Angela Lobo, Cheryl Lobo Jackson, my wonderful parents and sister, thank you for nurturing and teaching me all these years. Your hard work and sacrifices are greatly appreciated. I am blessed to have you as family.

And finally, my LORD, thank you for redeeming me and for allowing me to experience your true riches. You are truly magnificent, and I stand amazed at your beauty. There is nothing in this world that can even begin to compare to you, nothing!

Table of Contents

Introduction

Welcome to *Reclaiming Your Joy*! I am so excited that you have decided to take this journey with me. I know that God will bless our time together and will reveal some amazing truths to you about joy as you study his Word and deepen your relationship with him. I cannot even begin to tell you the passion I have for God's Word and its transforming power in our lives. *I came to a relationship with Christ by reading God's Word.* Let me digress for a moment and share a little about how the amazing power of God's Word changed my life and brought me true joy.

When I was in college, I met my husband, Shawn, who was a Christian. At the time, I did not have a personal relationship with Jesus Christ even though I attended church. Over time, my husband and I discussed spiritual things, but I was confused by the different religious systems. How could I know truth? Was truth relative? Why should I believe one religious system over another? As I sought to discover truth, I felt like I faced a wearisome and overwhelming struggle.

In anguish and desperation, I finally cried out to the LORD. I asked him to show me the truth if I read the Bible. So I sat down and read the Bible cover to cover. By the time I finished reading it, I knew that I was a sinner before a holy God and that Jesus was the atoning sacrifice for my sins. I also knew that salvation was through faith and not works, a free gift of God. Soon, I surrendered my life to Jesus Christ and accepted him as my LORD and Savior. I had been in such darkness and now was in such beautiful light. Because

I was saved by reading the Bible, I have a tremendous passion for the Word and its ability to change our lives and to bring us true joy.

Reclaiming Your Joy is an eight-week Bible study centered on the topic of joy. Each week covers a different aspect of joy or discusses some of the common joy-stealers, like worry, people, disappointment, and unforgiveness. Each week contains five days of homework, so if you have a crazy day (and we all have crazy days) and don't complete the homework, you will not fall behind in the study. The homework takes about thirty minutes to complete and allows you to study God's Word for yourself and to grow deeper in your faith. The homework includes a variety of questions, like fill-in-the-blank statements, multiple choice questions, yes/no questions, and matching questions. There are also exercises, which allow you to take the material and personally apply it to your life. All Scripture is based on the New International Version unless otherwise noted. I know that thirty minutes a day may seem daunting, but the result will be amazing. You will find a renewed passion in your relationship with God as he opens your eyes to the wonder of his truths. God has so much to share with us through his Word!

You can do *Reclaiming Your Joy* on an individual basis or as a group. If you do it as a group, there are suggested group questions, which can be found in the free Leaders Guide at www.captivated-bygod.org. These are only suggested questions, so please allow the Holy Spirit to direct and lead your group conversation. If you have more time and desire to go deeper into the Word, there are Challenge questions. There are also free audio lessons containing each week's topic at CaptivatedbyGod.org. So are you ready to reclaim your joy? Let's begin!

PART I:
Embracing Our Destinies

Week 1:
Our Great Calling

Day 1: The Cry of Scripture

Day 2: The Pursuit of Happiness

Day 3: The Fullness of Fellowship

Day 4: Whole-hearted Devotion

Day 5: Choosing Joy

Key Thoughts for the Week

Day 1: Scripture's resounding theme is that Christians should experience abundant, overflowing joy.

Day 2: Joy remains elusive for some of us because we do not pursue joy—we pursue happiness, that transitory feeling of fulfillment.

Day 3: The depth of joy we experience depends on the depth of our relationship with the LORD.

Day 4: A full relationship with the LORD means that we whole-heartedly devote ourselves to him and do not flirt with the world.

Day 5: No one takes our joy from us. We choose whether we will relinquish it because of a situation, person, or sin or whether we will cultivate and nurture it.

Day 1: The Cry of Scripture

Rejoice in the LORD always. I will say it again: Rejoice!

Philippians 4:4

C. S. Lewis wrote, "Joy is the serious business of Heaven."[1] It is also the serious business of earth. As Christians, we should live joy-filled lives. We should experience abundant, overflowing joy, and not just in isolated instances. But are we truly experiencing this type of joy? Or are we instead living day by day, struggling to get by, wearied and tired? If we are honest, we do not always experience the joy that Jesus so readily offered. Sometimes we live frustrated and discouraged lives, succumbing to the ways of the world and to Satan. The Christian walk sometimes seems more like a burden than a joy. Yet Jesus did not redeem us from our sin so that we would live miserable and downcast lives. He redeemed us so that we could be reconciled to the Father and experience abundant life through him. Abundant, overflowing joy is our birthright in Christ!

Compare joy with happiness.
Are happiness and joy the same thing? Explain.

_____

How does John 17:13 describe the joy that Christians should experience?

_____

What additional insight do you receive about joy from the following verses?

Romans 15:13_____

1 Peter 1:8 _____

How can joy serve as a witness for our Lord?

_____

Are you filled with full, inexpressible joy? Do others comment on your joy?

_____

As we speak of joy, it is important that we understand the difference between happiness and joy. We often use these words interchangeably, yet there is a great difference between them. Happiness is transient, momentary, and fleeting. It is dependent on the fulfillment of a need at a moment in time. If the need is not fulfilled, the feeling of happiness vanishes. Joy goes much deeper than happiness, for joy does not depend on our circumstances, feelings, or emotions. True joy is permanent and unchanging. It is a sense of well-being and peace that is unaffected by our external circumstances, an inner gladness of heart. For example, at the Last Supper, Jesus, knowing of his impending death, was able to sing hymns and praise to the Father (Mark 14:26). Jesus had a joy that was independent of his circumstances. The Lord does not promise us ease of circumstances but rather joy in the midst of our hardships and difficulties. Neither circumstances, nor trials, nor the world can steal our joy unless we let them, for joy is the triumph of eternity over the moment.

In John 17:13, Jesus offers his disciples full joy, not a partial joy dependent on people or a limited joy dependent on circumstances, but complete joy. First Peter 1:8 elaborates even further and describes joy as inexpressible. The Greek word translated _inexpressible_ means "unutterable."[2] Our joy bubbles forth so much that it overtakes us and is unutterable or unspeakable. That's a beautiful visual, isn't it? The world should stand amazed at the joy we possess. It should shock their senses because it is so contrary to the culture. Is this the type of joy we are experiencing—unutterable, shocking joy? Are others noticing our joy?

As we speak of joy, we must also remember that joy is expressed in many ways. Sometimes we express our joy through a burst of emotions, like shouting and singing, while at other times through quiet silence and prayer. Some people are naturally more expressive; hence their joy is more visual. This does not mean that the less expressive person is not experiencing joy, merely that it is displayed in a different form. Joy is not, however, walking around with an artificial smile all day. Some events in life, like the loss of a loved one, will break our hearts. Joy is not walking around with a forced smile during these times as if nothing has happened. Joy is the assurance of knowing our LORD is in control, will see us through the difficult time, and will bring good out of the situation.

Several years ago, my husband and I experienced a very difficult trial in our lives. Our twin boys were born prematurely at twenty eight weeks, weighing a little over two pounds each. They spent months in the hospital, fighting for their lives. It was a long, hard road for them and for us. Even when they finally came home, they still wore monitors for their breathing and had to have supplemental oxygen. Slowly over weeks and months, they gained strength and became healthy little boys. It was an incredibly difficult and challenging time for me. I could never have made it through this season in my life without the LORD. He carried me when I was physically exhausted, he loved me when I was emotionally overwhelmed, and he encouraged me when I was spiritually weak. He also provided me with his joy. During this time, I did not walk around with an artificial smile on my face, but I had a deep-seated peace and joy, knowing that God would help me and sustain me. This is what our LORD offers us – a supernatural joy that transcends the difficult circumstances of this life and enables us to not only endure the hardest of times but also to rejoice in them.

Who are three of the most joyful people that you know? What makes these people so joyful?

1. _____

2. _____

3. _____

What do the following Scriptures reveal about joy?

Psalm 32:11 _____

1 Thessalonians 5:16 _____

Romans 14:17 _____

Try to memorize Philippians 4:4.

_____ in the LORD _____.

I will say it again: _____ !

Challenge

How does a joyful heart overflow into the different parts of our lives? Match the verses with the appropriate answer.

_____ Psalm 122:1   A) give cheerfully and joyfully

_____ 2 Corinthians 9:7   B) joyfully accept the loss of property

_____ Philippians 1:3-4   C) rejoice in worship

_____ Hebrews 10:34   D) pray with joy

Joy is not an isolated act for us as Christians that we experience once a week, once a month, or after reaching a certain goal. We should experience joy consistently in our lives. "Rejoice in the LORD always. I will say it again: Rejoice!" (Philippians 4:4). No matter the circumstances of our lives, we should rejoice. Scripture does not tell us to rejoice only when we have a good-paying job, finally obtain the big house, reach a milestone, experience good health, receive recognition for our achievements, or have a house full of children. The resounding theme of Scripture is simply rejoice! Rejoice when you receive a promotion, and rejoice when you receive a demotion. Rejoice when you are rich, and rejoice when you are poor. Rejoice when you experience good health, and rejoice when you experience poor health. Rejoice, rejoice, rejoice. "But may the righteous be glad and rejoice before God; may they be happy and joyful" (Psalm 68:3).

As joy permeates our hearts, it naturally overflows into all of the different parts of our lives. The Greek word most commonly used for *joy* in the New Testament is *chara* and means "joy, rejoicing, gladness."[3] So our *chara*, our joy, becomes evident through our actions and spills forth into the various areas of our lives. For example, when we give, we give joyously. When we serve, we serve with gladness. When we pray, we pray joyfully.

Now that we have spent a few minutes to better understand what true joy is, how do we obtain it, and why does it seem so elusive at times? How can we learn to rejoice always, even in the darkest of circumstances? Can we really experience lives filled with such inexpressible joy that our community notices and is awed by our LORD? This study will help us to better understand how to obtain *consistent* joy in our lives and the various things that can hinder it.

Exercise

To help us better determine why our joy fluctuates, let's keep a joy journal in which we list three or four different activities for each day and how they affect our joy level.

Date	Event	Level of Joy (0 - joyless, 5 - joyful)
_____	_____	_____
_____	_____	_____
_____	_____	_____

Day 2: The Pursuit of Happiness

> "Meaningless! Meaningless!" says the Teacher. "Utterly meaningless! Everything is meaningless."
>
> Ecclesiastes 1:2

One of the reasons that joy sometimes seems elusive to us is because we do not pursue joy—we pursue happiness, that transitory feeling of fulfillment. We may inadvertently seek happiness in relationships, work, education, hobbies, entertainment, sports, and in so many other areas.

Few people in Scripture better depict the pursuit of happiness than King Solomon. He was the tenth son of King David and the third king of Israel and reigned for forty years around 1,000 BC. Although King David's reign encompassed much war and fighting, Solomon reigns during a time of unparalleled peace and prosperity. Scripture describes King Solomon as having greater riches and wisdom than all the other kings of the earth at the time. He also has a sizable harem and numerous wives. Yet with all his wealth, wisdom, and women, he does not seem to enjoy his life. In fact, he characterizes much of his life as "Meaningless! Meaningless!... Utterly meaningless! Everything is meaningless" (Ecclesiastes 1:2). Let's explore some of the different areas in which King Solomon seeks fulfillment.

Read Ecclesiastes 1:12-18. Where does King Solomon seek fulfillment? Does he find it?

_____

Have you ever sought fulfillment through intellectual pursuits? What about in your spiritual journey—are you driven to acquire more Bible knowledge or to really learn more about God?

_____

King Solomon has the unique distinction of being the wisest king in Scripture, other than our LORD Jesus. Over his lifetime, he composes over three thousand proverbs and writes over one thousand songs (1 Kings 4:32). He is wiser than anyone who has ruled before him in Jerusalem and obtains such a reputation that rulers from other distant nations seek him out to witness his wisdom (1 Kings 10:1-13). And yet, with all his wisdom and learning, Solomon learns that joy and fulfillment is not found in the acquisition of pure facts and knowledge. Philosophy and human knowledge do little to fulfill the void in our hearts. In fact, knowledge without love has the potential to create pride in us (1 Corinthians 8:1).

King Solomon's quest for knowledge still challenges many of us today. Just because we do not seek fulfillment through intellectual pursuits does not mean that we can easily dismiss this application. What about our spiritual journey? As we sit in our quiet times, are we trying to learn more facts, or do we truly desire to draw closer to God? Are we anticipating that God will reveal a new truth to us so that we can appear more spiritual before others? Bible knowledge can have the unsavory habit of creating a spiritual pride in us. We cannot let Satan deceive us. Even in Christian circles, we can easily substitute seeking God for seeking the knowledge of God. We can slowly and subtly became more enamored with the possession of God's knowledge than with the possession of God himself.

What do you learn about King Solomon's pursuit of pleasure from Ecclesiastes 2:1-3, 8-11 and 1 Kings 11:1-3? Does his pursuit of pleasure fulfill him?

_____

Is it wrong to seek fulfillment *only* through pleasure? Explain.

_____

King Solomon also seeks joy and fulfillment in pleasure—through women and alcohol. He denies himself nothing and refuses his heart no pleasure, but in the end, he is left empty and unfulfilled.

We too sometimes pursue pleasure in many avenues but forget to seek fulfillment in our Lord. And our desire for pleasure is not always in such destructive things as pornography, drugs, illicit sex, and alcohol; sometimes it comes prettily packaged through our hobbies, entertainment, and relationships. But seeking pleasure in things as innocuous as our hobbies can be just as destructive to our spiritual life as pursuing drugs. Both subtly distract us from the only one who can provide lasting joy. We must remember that the nature of pleasure is always transitory. It is gone as quickly as it comes. Please understand that I am not saying that we cannot enjoy things like hobbies or friendships; we certainly can, and God has given many of them to us as a gift, but they should not become the focus of our lives. None should take precedence over him or distract us from his sweet embrace. Those who truly seek and love God will in the end enjoy some of the pleasures of this life but will be filled because they have sought the true giver of pleasure and not just the pleasure itself.

Read 1 Kings 10:23 and Ecclesiastes 2:4-11. Where does King Solomon next seek fulfillment? Does he find it?

_____

Have you sought fulfillment through money and possessions? As you have achieved your financial goals, have you become content or created new financial goals?

_____

King Solomon also possesses incomparable wealth and prosperity—magnificent homes, vineyards, gardens, large flocks, and vaults overflowing with gold. He surpasses all the other kings and rulers in his wealth. He even possesses the funds to ensure that the smallest of his whims are met. King Solomon has the best of everything, yet his wealth does not bring him joy and fulfillment.

We must divest ourselves from the illusion that money and possessions will fulfill us. They will not. Though money and possessions can appear to satisfy us, they do so only superficially. They will never satisfy us in the long run, but Satan is only too happy to dangle his enticing bait before us—a bigger house, a nicer car, furnishings for the house, stylish new clothes, the large television set, the latest technological gadget. But the things of this world only satisfy for a moment. For example, a new car is never as exciting five years after the initial purchase. And what about all those lottery winners? Most of their lives could testify to the fact that money has not brought them true joy; quite the opposite has happened. Many of them have ended up downcast and miserable. But in our minds, we discount their testimony, don't we, thinking that if we were the lottery winner, the money would make us joyful. But is that true? As we have achieved our previous financial goals, has it made us more joyful, or have we instead only created newer financial goals?

If we remain focused on money and possessions, they will end up stealing far too much of our time. We will waste countless hours, months, and years being superficially satisfied. The LORD is the only one who can ever truly satisfy us, surpassing all we could ever imagine. C. S. Lewis aptly remarked, "Aim at Heaven and you will get earth 'thrown in': aim at earth and you will get neither."[4]

Read 1 Kings 6:1-2 and Ecclesiastes 2:17-26. Where does King Solomon finally seek fulfillment? Does he find it?

_____

Have you sought fulfillment by trying to obtain promotions and ascending the corporate ladder? What about trying to make a name for yourself at church or through volunteer activities? Explain.

_____

King Solomon also seeks joy and fulfillment through his work and his projects. He accomplishes a great deal in his lifetime and makes a name for himself. But in the end, this does not fulfill him. Spending countless hours working late and weekends in order to reach the next rung in the corporate ladder will not satisfy us. Though power and prestige may intoxicate us for a moment, in the end they will leave us disappointed and disillusioned. On the other hand, if we allow God to remain at the heart of our work, we will enjoy him and also our work.

Seeking fulfillment through work does not only apply to secular jobs; we can also seek earthly accomplishment within the church. Ministers, for example, can be just as prone to wanting to make a name for themselves as a CEO of a Fortune 500 company. And as lay persons, we can easily succumb to the desire for power or prestige— to lead committees or have the biggest Bible study classes. Wanting to make a name for ourselves, though concealed through spiritual terms, makes our desire for power and notoriety no less acceptable. Seeking God, for any other reason than himself, is wrong.

Having studied King Solomon, does it surprise you that a person could have wisdom, power, pleasure, sexual fulfillment, prestige, and wealth and yet still not be fulfilled? Be honest. Deep in the recesses of our hearts, we believe that somehow if we had all that Solomon had, we would be joyous and fulfilled; even if we had a small portion of what he possessed, we think we would be joyous. We must not believe Satan's subtle whisperings that the things of this world will satisfy us in the long run. They will not. We can only find true joy and fulfillment in our LORD, for he has set eternity in our hearts (Ecclesiastes 3:11). Blaise Pascal said, "There is a God shaped vacuum in the heart of every man which cannot be filled by any created thing, but only by God." Let me stress again that the LORD has graciously given us *all* things to enjoy, like money, hobbies, and even work, but none of these can be fully enjoyed unless the LORD resides at the heart of them.

Joy remains elusive for some of us today because we continue to seek fulfillment in the temporary and passing things of this world. We long for joy and inadvertently satiate ourselves in the wrong things. In the process, our joy goes up, then down, then up again, and then down again. We must be willing to surrender our transitory pleasures for more lasting ones. Let us learn from the experiences of King Solomon and not waste countless hours pursuing a happiness that will never truly fulfill. Let us seek refuge and comfort in the arms of our loving Father.

Exercise

Update your joy journal for the past day.

Date	Event	Level of Joy (0 - joyless, 5 - joyful)
_____	_____	_____
_____	_____	_____
_____	_____	_____

Day 3: The Fullness of Fellowship

O God, you are my God, earnestly I seek you; my soul thirsts for you, my body longs for you, in a dry and weary land where there is no water.

Psalm 63:1

The depth of our joy often depends on the depth of our relationship with the LORD. The stronger our relationship with the LORD, the greater the joy we experience. Since our relationship with the LORD plays such a vital role to our joy, we will spend the rest of today and all of tomorrow assessing it.

Read Genesis 18:16-25 and James 2:23, which describe Abraham's relationship with God and answer the following questions.

How does James 2:23 describe Abraham?_____

What does it take to cultivate a friendship? _____

What does the LORD reveal to Abraham?_____

What does the LORD do for his servants (Amos 3:7)?

_____

How does God's revelation to Abraham reveal the depth of their friendship?

_____

In the Old Testament, Abraham possessed the notable distinction of being called the friend of God. What a wonderful title—to be known as the friend of God. Think for a moment what that title denotes—love, companionship, warmth, caring, intimacy, fellowship. They talked, they trusted, they enjoyed each other's presence. Abraham's close friendship with the LORD is evidenced by the fact that the LORD approached Abraham and shared his plan of Sodom's judgment with him. "The LORD confides in those who fear him; he makes his covenant known to them" (Psalm 25:14). And then the LORD allowed Abraham to plead on Sodom's behalf. Can you imagine the LORD coming to you and telling you of his intention to judge a whole city? This reveals the depth of fellowship that Abraham possessed with our LORD, a friendship borne of love and obedience.

According to John 15:14-15, who has God also described as his friends? How does this encourage you?

_____

Evaluate your existing relationship with God. How well do you know and love him? Circle the word that best describes your relationship.

Acquaintance   Casual Friend   Best Friend

Is anything currently hindering you in your relationship with God?
☐ Excitement for other things   ☐ Lack of time
☐ Unwillingness to do God's will ☐ Known sin/disobedience
☐ Busyness   ☐ Lack of submission

As Christians living today, we also have the privilege of being called God's friends. "I no longer call you servants, because a servant does not know his master's business. Instead, I have called you friends, for everything that I learned from my Father I have made known to you" (John 15:15). What an amazing privilege that the God of this universe would call us his friends! We can experience the same level and depth of friendship that Abraham experienced. Isn't that exciting? If you are not currently experiencing this type of relationship, then start with a simple prayer and ask the LORD to help you love him more. God is faithful and will help us to love him—we need only ask.

What do you learn about the Word of God in Hebrews 4:12?

_____

What must the Word do in us (Colossians 3:16)? Why?

_____

Are you spending time with the LORD *daily* to cultivate your friendship with him? Circle the word that best describes your time commitment to the LORD.

Sometimes   Often   Always

If you are not spending time *daily* with the LORD, then do you need to make a change?

_____

The more we know and love God, the greater the joy that we experience. But we must be willing to make the time to know God. Though we may read a devotional occasionally and hear a sermon, we must spend time in the Word daily. Colossians 3:16 tells us to allow the Word to dwell in us richly. The word *dwell* means "to make one's home" or "to be at home."[5] How at home is the Word of God in us?

As we spend time in the Word of God, we will find that it has many wonderful benefits:

- The Word guides and directs us. It is hard to successfully navigate the waters of this life without the Word of God to guide us. It illuminates our path (Proverbs 6:23).

- The Word encourages us and helps build our faith. During times of difficulty and hardship, the LORD provides much needed strength and encouragement through his Word (Psalm 119:28).

- The Word provides us wisdom and instruction. We sometimes succumb to the world's wisdom because we are not grounded in God's wisdom. And yet God repeatedly tells us that the world's wisdom is foolishness. In following it, we will make costly mistakes and travel down paths we should not go (Proverbs 8:10-11).

- The Word teaches and trains us in righteousness so that we are equipped to do God's work. Through the Word, God helps us to understand about sin, salvation, and eternity. He also explains the Christian walk, spiritual warfare, and how to live victoriously in him (2 Timothy 3:16-17).

- The Word helps us to discern right from wrong and truth from falsehood. As we better understand the difference between right and wrong, we can make better choices.

- The Word also judges our thoughts and attitudes, correcting and rebuking us when necessary (Hebrews 4:12).

The greatest benefit of all, however, is that the Word enables us to know God and thus more fully rejoice in our Christian walk. From Genesis to Revelation, the Bible is the revelation of God to us. The LORD chose to reveal himself to us through the Bible—he did not have to tell us about himself at all but graciously chose to do so. Let's make use of this wonderful opportunity to truly know him.

Let me also caution that the Scriptures we learn must penetrate our hearts and transform us. We are not merely acquiring facts about God to be considered "learned." We are learning about God so that to every degree we become transformed and stand in awe of the only one who is truly worthy. If all our Bible studies and quiet times do not enable us to know God more fully and thus stand more amazed in his presence, then something is terribly wrong.

Read Psalm 63:1-3. Is the LORD your joy and delight? If you need to deepen your intimacy, then ask the LORD to help you love him more.

Challenge:

Read Exodus 33:12-23. For what does Moses ask? Have you ever asked God to reveal his glory to you? What happened?

A deep relationship with the LORD does not happen over night. It takes time and energy for us to develop our relationship with the LORD. If, for example, I only talked to my husband once a week, it would greatly hinder our relationship. It is only in talking with him and spending time with him daily that our relationship grows and matures. The same holds true for our relationship with the LORD. We must be willing to invest the necessary time with our LORD. If we spend this life snacking on the LORD, listening to a few sermonettes here and there and reading a couple of devotionals, then we will miss our true feast. If we have to sacrifice other things in our lives due to our busy schedules, like shopping or watching television, then let's sacrifice them; but let us never sacrifice our sweet communion with our LORD. These are the most important and most significant times in our life.

Psalm 63:1 says, "O God, you are my God, earnestly I seek you; my soul thirsts for you, my body longs for you, in a dry and weary land where there is no water." These are passionate words from the psalmist, aren't they? But what about us? Are we earnestly seeking him? Do our souls thirst for him? Do we spend enough time with our LORD to stand transfixed by his beauty and amazed by his majesty? If not, then let's ask our LORD to help us love him deeply and passionately, for he is truly magnificent.

Exercise

Update your joy journal for the past day.

Date	Event	Level of Joy (0 - joyless, 5 - joyful)
_____	_____	_____
_____	_____	_____
_____	_____	_____

Day 4: Whole-hearted Devotion

> No one can serve two masters. Either he will hate the one and love the other, or he will be devoted to the one and despise the other. You cannot serve both God and Money.
>
> Matthew 6:24

A full relationship with the LORD means that we whole-heartedly devote ourselves to him. But sometimes we flirt with the world and with the LORD, squandering our affections. We place God in our lives but leave him in the midst of a sea of other gods, like the god of work, the god of television, the god of shopping, the god of friendship. Unfortunately, these other gods subtly divide our allegiance and secretly steal our devotion. A divided allegiance will cripple our Christian walk and leave us at an elementary level of joy at best and many times not even that.

According to 1 John 2:15-17, what should we not love? Why?

_____

What additional warnings are we given in the following verses?

James 4:4_____

Who was Demas (Philemon 1:24), and what happened to him as a result of his love for the world (2 Timothy 4:10)?

Read Psalm 86:11-12. List anything that is currently dividing your affection for the LORD. Do you need to ask the LORD for an undivided heart to love him?

Matthew 6:24 reminds us that *no one* can serve two masters. Either we will "hate the one and love the other, or [we] will remain devoted to one and despise the other." Though Matthew 6:24 focuses specifically on mammon, which refers to material goods and possessions, there is an underlying theme—we cannot serve two masters. For example, we cannot serve our LORD and the god of our career. We cannot serve our LORD and the god of our possessions. God wants our complete devotion.

One of Satan's greatest techniques is not to make us hate God but rather to help us "forget" him amidst all the enticing offerings of this world. Satan keeps us oblivious to the wonders of God, and we move day to day, week to week without actively pursuing God. Slowly the weeks become months, and the months turn into years, and before we know it, we have squandered our affections. Ultimately, whatever relationship we choose to spend our time and energy on will grow and flourish. If we spend our time and energy with the LORD, then we help nurture and grow that relationship. On the other hand, if we devote our time and energy to worldly things, then we will cultivate and develop those relationships. As this happens, we will no longer crave spiritual things because our worldly appetites will begin to take over. As we entertain these other little gods in our lives, they subtly dull our desire for our true LORD without us ever realizing it. I am sure that when Demas started out, he never believed that he would end up with a lukewarm relationship with the LORD. Paul initially considered him one of his fellow co-workers (Philemon 1:24). But in the end, Demas loved the world too much and his LORD too little (2 Timothy 4:10). What a warning for us about feeding our earthly appetites. None of us starts out by saying that we want a lukewarm relationship with our LORD, but if we do not wisely invest time with him, that is how we could end up. In the end, our choices either draw us closer to God or take us farther away.

The little gods of our life also make an awful master. For instance, if we pursue success in our career at the expense of our relationship with the LORD, we may soon find ourselves enslaved by success, placing it before the LORD and our family. Before we know it, our careers begin to consume more and more of our time. Through it all, we tell ourselves that one day we will develop our relationship with God… one day we will pursue him… one day we will taste his delights. But one day never comes because we have been blinded by the god of this world to the true things of God. We cannot allow Satan to deceive us—the offerings of this world will never bring us true freedom and joy. Only the LORD provides that. Again, we must remember that it is not that these things are inherently bad but rather that they cannot truly be enjoyed apart from God.

In our minds, we sometimes think that we can love the LORD and still love our little gods at the same time. But we are mistaken, and the price is far greater than we could ever imagine—a half-hearted, lukewarm relationship with the LORD. And a half-hearted relationship will result in half-hearted joy as we waver between highs and lows. C. S. Lewis said,

> …it would seem that our LORD finds our desires not too strong, but too weak. We are half-hearted creatures, fooling

about with drink and sex and ambition when infinite joy is offered us, like an ignorant child who wants to go on making mud pies in a slum because he cannot imagine what is meant by the offer of a holiday at the sea. We are far too easily pleased. [6]

We are far too easily pleased by the things of this world, settling for its measly scraps instead of feasting with our Master. But why thirst for that which cannot fill and hunger for that which cannot satiate (Isaiah 55:1-2)? Why not satiate ourselves in the LORD instead and find true fulfillment in him? "Taste and see that the LORD is good" (Psalm 34:8a). We must zealously guard our relationship with the LORD. Many distracters will seek to ensnare us, but nothing, not the career, not the hobby, not the material possession, this world offers us is worth even a temporary diversion—nothing.

Read Acts 19:17-20. What do these Christians do? Why?

_____

Fill in the blanks - Philippians 3:8.
    What is more, I consider _____ a _____ compared to _____, for whose sake I have lost all things. I consider them _____ that I may gain Christ.

Honestly assess yourself. Is there something that you will not sacrifice to the LORD, like possessions, comfort, reputation, or security?

_____

Sometimes we possess a half-hearted relationship because we will not surrender certain aspects of our lives. In Acts 19, some Christians confess their practices of sorcery and then burn their scrolls. Do not casually pass by the next verse—the value of the scrolls is sizable, fifty thousand drachmas. A drachma was a silver coin that was comparable to a day's wage. Thus, fifty thousand drachmas is fifty thousand days' wages for an average laborer. Can you imagine the astonishing value of what these Christians destroy? Yet these Christians do not cling to their scrolls as a keepsake or sell them for profit. They burn them because of their evilness. Every earthly possession is nothing compared to our relationship with God. "What is more, I consider everything a loss compared to the surpassing greatness of knowing Christ Jesus my Lord, for whose sake I have lost all things. I consider them rubbish, that I may gain Christ" (Philippians 3:8). Paul considers everything that he has lost as rubbish. The Greek word translated *rubbish* is *skubalon* and means "that which is thrown to the dogs, dregs, refuse, what is thrown away as worthless. Spoken of the refuse of grain, chaff, or of a table, of slaughtered animals, of dung."[7] Paul considers all things, not some things, not most things, but all things that he lost nothing more than dung. Is that how we view the things that we have lost in our lives—as nothing more than dung?

Someone once remarked that we must sometimes destroy that which has earthly value in order to preserve that which has eternal value. Are we willing to take such stringent measures in our relationship with the Lord? Would we destroy the scrolls, or would we compromise? In our Christian walk, are we willing to burn whatever is holding us back? We cannot turn over 95 percent of our lives to the Lord and keep the other 5 percent secret. The Lord wants all 100 percent. Let's pause for a moment and see if we are holding anything back.

- Am I willing to forsake all, including my family and friends, for Christ?

- Do I read my Bible with as much excitement and zeal as I read other publications, surf the internet, or text my friends?

- Am I spending significant time every day communing with the LORD through prayer? Is my prayer time a pleasure or a burden?

- Am I more excited about living on this earth or about eternity with my LORD?

These are hard questions. They challenge us to the core, and sometimes the answers are not what we would like. If we are honest, we all sometimes prefer television to reading our Bible or meeting up with friends to praying. And yet we cannot shy away from answering such questions. It is only in acknowledging that we are not where we would like to be that we can grow in our relationship with the LORD. God does not expect perfection from us but a willingness to turn to him for help. He will always meet us where we are. Let's ask the LORD to pierce our hearts for him and to shatter any veneers of superficiality. Then we will stand, as many have stood before us, awed by his magnificent presence.

Joy is the overflow of our relationship with the LORD. We will never have true, abundant joy if we do not know and love God passionately. We were made for something far greater than this world. Let's stop settling. Let's stop playing with the world and start loving God whole-heartedly; then we will experience a joy we could never imagine.

Exercise

Update your joy journal for the past day.

Date	Event	Level of Joy (0 - joyless, 5 - joyful)
_____	_____	_____
_____	_____	_____
_____	_____	_____

Day 5: Choosing Joy

> No one will take away your joy.
>
> John 16:22b

In the past few days, we have been exploring the basic nature of joy. We have discussed 1) what joy truly is, 2) how we sometimes pursue happiness instead of joy, and 3) how a deeper relationship with God allows us to deepen our joy. Now that we better understand the nature of joy, let's spend some time reflecting on our view of God's nature and on our current level of joy.

Take a few minutes and reflect on your view of God.

Do you view God as joyous?_____

Do you picture God smiling? Why or why not? _____

Do you think Jesus laughed? Explain. _____

What do you learn about God from the following Scriptures?

Psalm 104:31 _____

Isaiah 65:18-19 _____

In the parable of the Talents in Matthew 25:14-30, what did the Master tell the two faithful servants (Matthew 25:21, 23)? Does that surprise you?

_____

Do you think God wants you to experience joy in your life?

Ecclesiastes 8:15 _____

Sometimes we picture God as a hard and sullen task master; thus we expect the same in our lives. But God is joyous. He is not some cosmic killjoy. Do you picture him like that? Do you envision God smiling and rejoicing? God rejoices over his creation (Psalm 104:31) and over us (Isaiah 65:18-19, Zephaniah 3:17). In the parable of the talents, for example, the master entrusts three of his servants with talents. Upon his return, he inspects their work. To two of them, he responds, "Well done, good and faithful slave. You were faithful with a few things, I will put you in charge of many things; enter into the joy of your master" (Matthew 25:23, NASB). Did you catch the last part of the master's statement—*"enter into the joy of your master."* The master has great joy and the master represents our LORD.

When Jesus walked this earth, I do not think that he spent every moment in rigid stoicism. He laughed, he fellowshipped, he enjoyed life. Many of the Jewish ritual offerings and feasts were meant to be joyful celebrations as the people remembered their great blessings. The LORD wants us also to remain joyful, to delight in our families, to celebrate our salvation, and to rejoice in fellowshipping with others. "This is the day the LORD has made; let us rejoice and be glad in it" (Psalm 118:24).

Earlier in the week, you were asked to maintain a joy journal to help you better determine what is affecting your joy. Please take a few minutes now and update your journal.

Exercise

Date	Event	Level of Joy (0 - joyless, 5 - joyful)
_____	_____	_____
_____	_____	_____
_____	_____	_____

LORRAINE HILL

Now that you have updated your journal, let's reflect on your joy level for the whole week. Please use your daily joy journal to answer the following questions.

What type of events tended to increase your joy?

_____

Did certain events decrease your joy? If so, describe them.

_____

Did you notice any triggers, like being at the end of the day, work, kids' tantrums?

_____

Did your joy tend to fluctuate with the circumstances in your life?
☐ Yes   ☐ No

If your "joy" fluctuated with the circumstances in your life, then was your joy dependent on the LORD or on your circumstances? Is this real joy?

_____

If you are like most of us, then you probably discovered that your joy was haphazard and inconsistent. It probably depended on the different circumstances that you encountered during the week. If most of the week progressed well, then you probably experienced a high level of joy. On the other hand, if circumstances seemed depressing and overwhelming, your joy level probably declined. So is this real joy? No. Real joy, true joy, should be consistent in our lives, independent of the various circumstances that we face. Since true joy comes from our LORD, we should be able to experience joy no matter the turmoil around us. So, for example, we can lose our job and yet still remain joyful. We can spend long hours in traffic and not get frustrated. We can do household chores and keep a joyous attitude. If we are honest, however, many of us experience a yo-yo or rollercoaster joy, up one moment and down the next.

Several years ago, as I was experiencing periods of joylessness, the LORD slowly revealed to me that my joy was not fully in him but rather in the circumstances around me. When circumstances went well, I experienced happiness; when circumstances went badly, I experienced misery. Slowly over time, I have learned to keep my focus more on the LORD and less on my circumstances so that I can now experience a more consistent level of joy. If you are experiencing a yo-yo or rollercoaster joy, spend some time with the LORD and determine the real cause. Could it be that you have sought joy in circumstances and in people instead of in the LORD and his fellowship?

Can anyone take our joy from us (John 16:22b)?
☐ Yes   ☐ No

Read John 10:10. What does the thief come to do? Mark those that apply.
☐ Steal   ☐ Kill   ☐ Destroy

According to John 10:10b, what does Jesus offer us?
I have come that they may have _____, and have it to _____.

Can you think of some ways that Satan seeks to steal your joy?

_____

Let me reiterate again that the LORD's great desire for us is to experience joy—abundant, lasting, inexpressible joy. If we are experiencing anything less than this, we are living below our great calling. Though the Christian walk certainly has challenges and obstacles, the LORD sufficiently enables us to bear anything that comes our way and more importantly provides us a deep-seated joy, even during the worst of hardships or persecution. That is what makes Christian joy supernatural. Let's not look to the world or even to other Christians and assume such joy is unattainable—it is. Thousands of Christians over the years can testify that joy is not only attainable but is easily accessible, even in the face of great adversity.

As much as the LORD desires for us to experience consistent joy in our lives, so Satan seeks to steal it. He will do anything he can to destroy our joy. He will whisper sweet nothings in our ears and incite bitterness, worry, envy, and a whole host of other things in us. He will try to discourage and dishearten us. He will try to make us forget our LORD.

John 16:22 reminds us that no one can take our joy from us. We choose whether we relinquish it because of a situation, person, or sin or whether we cultivate and nurture it. We choose whether we allow our circumstances, our very temporary circumstances, to determine our level of joy. We do not want to merely endure this life; we want to triumph in it. So let us choose joy and live up to our great calling. "May the God of hope fill you with all joy and peace as you trust in him, so that you may overflow with hope by the power of the Holy Spirit" (Romans 15:13).

Week 2:
Abiding Joy

Day 1: A Natural Fruit

Day 2: Simple Obedience

Day 3: Ensnared by Rules

Day 4: The Freedom to Flourish

Day 5: Seduced by Sin

Key Thoughts for the Week

Day 1: Joy is a fruit of the Spirit, produced naturally in us as we abide in Christ.

Day 2: Obedience is the gateway that opens the flood gates of joy to us.

Day 3: Legalism is death to the Christian walk for it makes the Christian walk harsh and demanding instead of exciting and joyous.

Day 4: Because legalism grows slowly and subtly, it can easily creep into our lives if we do not diligently guard against it.

Day 5: Whenever we choose to sin, we are saying yes to a momentary satisfaction and no to lasting joy; we are choosing an earthly pleasure over an eternal fulfillment.

Day 1: A Natural Fruit

> But the fruit of the Spirit is... joy
>
> Galatians 5:22

Last week we discussed the nature of joy and our existing level of joy. If you were not able to complete Week 1, please finish it before starting this week. Week 1 is foundational to this study and explores some basic ideas about joy. We will draw on these basic ideas throughout the rest of this study.

What do you learn about joy from Galatians 5:22-23?

_____

Based on Galatians 5:22-23, who creates joy in our lives?
☐ We do   ☐ the Holy spirit   ☐ the world

Have you ever seen someone try to artificially create joy in his life? What happened? How is this different than when the Holy Spirit produces joy in our lives?

_____

Joy is a fruit of the Spirit that is produced naturally in us as we abide in God. Once we accepted Jesus as our LORD and Savior, we were indwelt with the Holy Spirit. The Holy Spirit produces spiritual fruit in us, like the fruit of joy. Though we may sometimes try to manufacture joy in our lives, we usually end up with fake fruit, superficial smiles that never quite penetrate our hearts. Rather than trying to create our own joy, we need to accept and cultivate the joy the LORD has already provided for us. We cultivate the fruit of joy and allow it to blossom by deepening our relationship with God, obeying his commands, and submitting to his Word. On the other hand, we can wither the fruit by grieving the Holy Spirit, keeping known sin in our lives, or disobeying the LORD.

Did you notice that joy is listed second in Galatians 5:22-23? Are you surprised by its prominence? Joy is second only to the virtue of love, which lies at the heart of the Christian walk. This underlies the importance of joy in our lives. The LORD does not want us to live downcast and miserable lives, but rather to rejoice in him and to experience consistent joy in our lives.

Read John 15:1-11. What does Jesus tell us in John 15:5?

_____

What does it mean to abide in the LORD (John 15:7, 10)?

_____

What is the result of abiding in our LORD (John 15:11)?

_____

Do you regularly abide in the LORD? Circle the answer that best describes you.

Often   Sometimes   Rarely

If you did not answer Often, then is there something you need to change in order to regularly abide?

_____

Producing fruit (having and maintaining joy) is not some laborious, arduous process. It is the result of us remaining or abiding in our LORD. Jesus uses the word *abide* eleven times in this John 15 passage in order to stress the importance of us abiding or remaining in him. We abide in God, and he produces joy in us. What does it mean to abide in our LORD? Abiding means to regularly dwell with the

Lord and to obey his commands. It can entail reading the Word, listening to the Lord, praying, and serving him. Abiding does not mean that we are perfect and never sin but rather that we repent and confess our sin to our Lord, thus continuing in our fellowship with him.

What are three of your greatest challenges for living a *daily* joyous life?

1. _____ 2. _____ 3. _____

Does the commonness of life ever seem to strip your joy?

☐ Yes, frequently   ☐ Yes, occasionally   ☐ No, never

How can focusing on your eternal reward enable you to remain more joyous today?

Galatians 6:9-10 _____

Hebrews 6:9-12 _____

What are some unique ways that you have remained joyous during your daily routine?

_____

Now that we have learned about the importance of abiding in our Lord, let's discuss a practicality—how to live a joyous life *daily*. Earlier you were asked to list some of your greatest challenges to joy. If we are honest, one of our greatest challenges is that the commonness of life strips the joy right from us. Somehow cleaning the toilets, mowing the yard, and sitting at a desk at work are not events that typically inspire great joy in us. Yet the Lord desires for us to remain joyful in *all* circumstances. The greatness of our calling as Christians is not that we experience one amazing moment after another and therefore remain joyous. It is instead that we find joy in the ordinary, that we rejoice while performing the common tasks of life, like changing diapers or going to work.

So how can we remain joyful while performing ordinary tasks?

- First, as we discussed earlier today, we need to abide in our LORD. Then, the commonness of life will not bother us as much. If we are out of fellowship and focused on ourselves, even the most minor things will seem to bother us.

- Second, we must focus on our relationship with the LORD and the joy of knowing him for it will eclipse any minor displeasure that we may face, like mopping the floors or raking the yard. Perhaps to help us remain focused on the LORD, we can turn on some praise music. Before we know it, the boring, mundane tasks are completed, and we have enjoyed a special time of worship with our LORD.

- Third, we must cultivate a thankful spirit. As we become more thankful for God's gracious provision to us, we will remain more joyous. Since we will devote all of Week 8 to discussing thankfulness, we will not explore it further here.

- Fourth, we can post favorite Bible verses in conspicuous places. As we see the Bible verses, they will remind us to remain focused on the LORD and on the things of eternity. This helps us keep a proper *eternal* perspective so that we can remain joyous doing the more mundane tasks of life.

- Fifth and finally, we must view whatever task we are performing as significant. We sometimes mistakenly view the visible or more prominent service as somehow better than the hidden places of service, like serving as an administrator or cleaning the church. We want God to do great things in our lives, noticeable things, but all tasks, if done to the glory of God, are important and bear a reward in eternity. For example, though changing diapers may not seem significant, we must view the task as important because it allows us to take care of our child. Sometimes it is easy to become so lost in the details that we forget the big picture. We cannot listen to Satan's deceitful whispers that our ordinary, commonplace tasks are useless. They are not. It is the godly person who joyfully performs his daily tasks and seeks no great ministry for himself, only honor for his Lord. So consider that third load of dishes or that late project your boss gives you as a special fragrant offering to the Lord, your sweet sacrifice of worship.

We sometimes live under the illusion that when a certain occurrence happens we will be joyous, but we miss the wonderful promise of God. Joy does not come tomorrow. Joy is here now if we will abide in him. Joy is here when we do that eighth load of laundry. Joy is here when our boss yells and demeans us. Joy is here when we sit wedged in traffic for two hours because of a wreck. Joy is here because, regardless of our earthly circumstances, we have infinite love and eternal life from the Creator of the universe. Joy is here even during the most mundane of tasks, if we will choose it.

Day 2: Simple Obedience

> I am the Lord's servant…May it be to me as you have said.
>
> Luke 1:38

Yesterday, we discussed the importance of abiding in our Lord in order to produce the fruit of joy in our lives. A key part of abiding involves obedience. As the Lord commands and directs us, we must choose to obey him.

Read Luke 1:26-38 about Mary's obedience to God and answer the following questions.

Why would Gabriel's announcement perplex Mary? _____

How does Gabriel encourage Mary? _____

How does Mary respond? _____

What do you think are some of the thoughts that raced through Mary's mind?

_____

Challenge

After her encounter with Gabriel, Mary offers a song of praise to the LORD, often called *Mary's Song* or *The Magnificat*. What parts of *Mary's Song* speak to your heart (Luke 1:46-55)?

_____

Share an instance in which obedience to God resulted in great joy.

_____

Mary, the mother of Jesus, was a Jew descended from the tribe of Judah. She is perhaps fifteen or sixteen at the time of Gabriel's visit and is a virgin, a fact Scripture twice states to emphasize her purity. She is also engaged to be married to Joseph, a carpenter in Nazareth.

As the LORD seeks to use Mary in his work, he sends the angel Gabriel to inform her of his plans. Upon seeing Mary, Gabriel tells Mary that she will give birth to a son and that he will be the Messiah. Mary is initially perplexed and troubled when Gabriel comes to her. It was rare for an angel to appear to a human being and even rarer for one to speak to a woman. Most people in Scripture who saw an angel were usually overcome by fear. Mary is also probably considering her existing engagement to Joseph. Jewish marriages during these times consisted of three steps, and the engagement phase was considered legally binding. It meant that the groom had paid the bride's price to the bride's family. It also meant that the groom had accepted responsibility for the bride, though they were not allowed to live together until the actual wedding occurred. Only a writ of divorce could break an engagement. Imagine Mary's thoughts as Gabriel announces God's plans for her life. Like many women of her day, she probably has visions of being married in a lovely ceremony and excited thoughts of her first year with Joseph, but God has a different idea.

Gabriel reassures Mary by providing more details of Jesus's conception and birth. He also explains that her relative Elizabeth is now pregnant with John the Baptist, the forerunner for Christ. Of all the women whom God could choose to be the mother of the forerunner for Christ, God chooses Elizabeth, someone Mary knows. What comfort this provides Mary. After all, once Mary becomes pregnant, few will believe that she has supernaturally conceived, but Elizabeth will understand. How nice for Mary to have a companion and confidante. Whenever the LORD places a great task before us, he always provides the support we need. Gabriel also reminds Mary that with God all things are possible. What great encouragement to us as well. No matter the situation we face, nothing is impossible with God.

Mary carefully listens and deliberates on what Gabriel tells her. Then she simply responds, "I am the LORD's servant...May it be to me as you have said" (Luke 1:38). The word translated *servant* means "a slave, one who is in a permanent relation of servitude to another, his will being altogether consumed in the will of the other."[1] Mary could have easily argued with God or tried to negotiate a more suitable timing for her life, perhaps after she and Joseph had been married for a while. Instead, she sets aside her dreams for the future and acquiesces to the LORD's plans for her life.

Describe obedience based on 1 Samuel 15:22.

_____

What are some of the reasons that you sometimes do not obey the Lord's will?

☐ Over-analyze the situation ☐ Lack of time
☐ Fear of the unknown ☐ Out of comfort level
☐ Inconvenient ☐ Too young or too old

According to Ephesians 5:15-17, how should we live? Why?

_____

Fill in the blanks - Psalm 40:8.

I desire to _____, O my God; your law is within my _____.

Mary's response is quite remarkable, isn't it? Let's review some things that she teaches us about obedience.

- Obedience should be immediate. Mary immediately obeys the Lord and does not try to negotiate with God for a more suitable timing. She does not get lost in the details or allow her pragmatism to hinder her obedience. She simply accepts his will and obeys him. I must also caution that delayed obedience is disobedience because we have failed to act in faith based on the Lord's timing. Imagine if Mary had said no. She would have lost a great blessing—having the Messiah. Obedience always leads to a blessing.

- Obedience encompasses all areas of our lives. Partial obedience, obeying some of God's commands while ignoring other commands, is not obedience. Second Corinthians 2:9 reminds us that we are to "be obedient in everything." A few years ago, my husband and I considered going to Africa as short-term missionaries. After patiently listening to me voice concerns about the political and social structure of the country, my husband asked a probing question. He said, "Lorraine, do you really want to be the one that stands before the LORD, not having done his will?" My husband certainly has the uncanny knack of speaking God's truth to me. But sometimes the uncertainties of life overcome me, and I need his gentle urging.

- Obedience may necessitate rearranging our plans and changing our vision. Mary allows the LORD to rearrange her plans for the future. She remains open to his leading even though it is costly and inconvenient. It is very inconvenient for Mary to place her marriage and a future with Joseph on hold. She will endure ridicule and mocking and will lose friendships. The LORD's plans are rarely convenient. He seems to give us opportunities when we are the busiest and when things seem the most hectic. But whose time do we hold in our hands—his or ours? We must not be unwise but understand what the LORD's will is and be obedient to it (Ephesians 5:15-17). We must learn to be flexible, willing to lay aside our dreams and visions for the future to do the LORD's will. And yet that is sometimes so hard, isn't it? We often already have a plan for the future; we know what we want. Instead, let us start our mornings on our knees and commit to do God's will each day. This can help us remain focused on him and his plans for us.

- Obedience should happen with a happy and cheerful disposition. Mary does not begrudgingly agree to the LORD's will. She fully accepts it and rejoices in it even though it will involve hardship and inconvenience. She even composes a spontaneous song of worship to the LORD.

- Obedience must also conquer fear. Sometimes God's will moves us into the unknown, where all comfort and security are removed. As Gabriel communicates God's will to Mary, she probably fears many things. What will her parents think? Will they disown her? And what about Joseph-will he divorce her? Will her friends stand by her? How will her life change? We cannot allow our fears to paralyze us but must perform the LORD's will. His power and grace are sufficient to overcome anything we face. "The LORD is my light and my salvation—whom shall I fear? The LORD is the stronghold of my life—of whom shall I be afraid?" (Psalm 27:1).

- Ultimately obedience is evidence of the state of our heart. It shows the depth of our love for the LORD. "If anyone loves me, he will obey my teaching…He who does not love me will not obey my teaching" (John 14:23-24). Mary loves the LORD and thus obeys his commands. *We can obey the Lord and not love him, but we cannot continually disobey the Lord and truly love him.*

Abiding in God involves our obedience and submission to God's will for our lives. It is complete surrender. We will never experience abundant, overflowing joy if we disobey our LORD. Obedience is the gateway that opens the floodgates of joy to us, a key that unlocks the chest of rejoicing.

Day 3: Ensnared by Rules

This is love for God: to obey his commands.
And his commands are not burdensome.
1 John 5:3

Sometimes in our misguided zeal for obedience, we create artificial standards of *dos* and *do nots*. We mistakenly think that conformance to these standards will enable us to live the Christian walk victoriously. What we fail to realize is that quite the opposite is true. These artificial standards bring defeat rather than victory and strip our joy rather than increasing it.

Read Galatians 1:6-7. What astonishes Paul?

_____

Of what must we be careful (Colossians 2:6-8)?

_____

What is legalism? Can you think of any legalistic rules that plague the church today?

_____

What should be the reason for our obedience (John 14:15)?

_____

The epistle of Galatians is affectionately referred to as the Magna Carta of Christian Liberty because it clearly states the foundation of salvation by faith and not by works. It also encourages us to be free in our Christian walk, rather than living under the heavy yoke of legalism. What is legalism? Legalism is adherence to an artificial system of rules, a system of *dos* and *do nots*, for either obtaining salvation or for growing in one's spiritual walk. Usually these rules are rigid and demanding, leaving little room for grace or the working of the Holy Spirit.

Legalism usually occurs when rules are created for grey areas in the Christian walk, areas not specified in the Bible. But legalism can also occur in a more subtle way, when one does things specified in Scripture but does them from the wrong motivation. Legalism places ritualism over love, in essence trying to formulize the Christian walk.

In Galatians 1, Paul admits that he is astonished that the people are so quickly deserting the grace of Christ and turning to a different gospel. In his commentary on Galatians, John MacArthur provides this insight.

> The Galatian Christians not only were being confused and weakened in their confidence to live by grace but were actually deserting. The term behind deserting (*metatithemi*) was used

of military desertion, which was punishable by death during time of war, much as in modern times... The false teachers were accountable for their corruption of God's truth, but the Galatian Christians were also accountable for being so easily misled by it to pursue legalism.[2]

The Galatian Christians are choosing to exchange liberty, true freedom in Christ, for legalism. And this *astonishes* Paul. Paul is astonished that people would leave a life of freedom and return to a life of bondage.

Legalism will squeeze the joy from our lives, drop by drop. In fact, joy is one of the first things we lose as we come back under legalism's bondage. Because we are constantly following manmade rules and artificial standards, our Christian walk soon becomes tiring and demanding. I think most of us would say that when we were first saved, we experienced a sweetness and an excitement to our Christian walk. But over time, do we still view the Christian walk as joyous, or does it now seem more like a burden? Slowly and subtly, without us ever realizing it, we may have succumbed to legalism, and in the process, our joy and excitement have slowly slipped away. Our Christian walk may seem like nothing more than rules, rules, and more rules.

Yet all these rules miss the heart of the Christian walk—love for our Lord. "This is love for God: to obey his commands. And his commands are not burdensome" (1 John 5:3). The Greek word *barus*, translated *burdensome*, means "grievous, meaning oppressive, hard to be borne, referring to precepts."[3] God's commands should not be oppressive or hard because they are done with a heart that overflows with love for God. If we perform all the rules of the Bible but miss the greatest rule, to love God, then we have missed everything. Legalism skews our relationship with God—we view God as a taskmaster instead of our loving Father; thus it produces obedience born from the wrong motives. It makes obedience a burden, rather than a delight, an obligation instead of a joy. And yet

Scripture repeatedly paints the picture of God as our loving father. He has compassion on his children, he nurtures them, he protects them, he loves them unconditionally. If we do not realize this, then we become performers to gain God's love.

What two main issues does Paul address in Galatians 2?

Galatians 2:1-10 _____

Galatians 2:11-16 _____

What affect does Peter's legalism have on those around him (Galatians 2:13)?

_____

What warning do we receive from 1 Corinthians 10:32? Are there any actions in your life currently that might be leading others astray?

_____

In Galatians 2, Paul addresses two main issues concerning legalism. First, the Judaizers, Jewish legalists, want to circumcise Titus, who is an uncircumcised, Gentile believer. The Judaizers taught that a Gentile had to be circumcised before becoming a Christian. Circumcision was considered the badge of faith for Jews. It was an important rite descended from Abraham, which distinguished them from pagans. In essence, the Judaizers want to impose Jewish laws on the Gentile Christians.

In order to settle the matter, the church leaders meet in Jerusalem, referred to as the Jerusalem Conference/Council (Acts 15). This conference affirms that Gentile believers do not need to be circumcised to be saved. Both Jews and Gentiles are saved by the same means—faith in Jesus Christ. Salvation was accomplished solely through Jesus's atoning work on the cross and does not require circumcision or any other act, like baptism or joining a particular church.

The second issue involves Peter's eating at only the Jewish table. Initially, Peter eats with the Gentiles and fellowships with them. But when certain Judaizers arrive and proclaim their rules, Peter withdraws from the Gentile believers and separates himself from them. Eating and fellowshipping with Gentiles was important because it symbolized unity in Christ, that the Jews and Gentiles were one family. Previously, Jews and Gentiles ate at separate tables because Orthodox Jews considered some of the Gentile food to be unclean. But salvation does not require that we eat or not eat certain foods. Thus, Paul openly rebukes Peter's actions in order to affirm the gospel and liberty in our Christian walk.

Peter allows his fear to get the better of him. He withdraws not because he is unaware of the Judaizers' legalistic rules, but rather because he is afraid of them. Peter allows his desire to please others to overcome him. We sometimes fall into the same snare, don't we? We go along with legalistic rules in order to please others and appease their pressure. Sometimes it is easier to follow the crowd than to stand up for righteousness, and yet God wants us to stand up for righteousness.

It is unfortunate that Peter's courage fails him and he succumbs to his fears. In doing so, he influences others negatively and leads them astray. As a leader in the community, Peter commands the respect and following of many. Thus, in his error, he causes others to err also. Even Barnabas, another strong church leader, follows him and yields to the Judaizers legalistic rules. We must be careful of how we act because our actions impact those around us. We want to lead others toward the LORD, not away from him.

Though the Judaizers' legalistic rules about circumcision and food may seem silly to us today, we are probably guilty of just as silly rules, born not out of Scripture but rather out of our traditions and preferences. Do any of these legalistic rules and judgments sound familiar?

- My denomination is the only true church.

- The King James Version is the only true Bible.

- Worship must be carried out in a certain way with a certain type of music.

- Good Christians should not own luxury items.

- Bible study should be done first thing in the morning.

- Watching movies or television shows makes you less spiritual.

Did you notice the resounding theme in these examples? In all these instances, rules have been created by standards not specified in Scripture. I must also caution that it is often easier to see legalism in others than it is to see it in ourselves.

It is easy to slowly fall into legalism, isn't it? Yet, legalism does nothing but slowly strip away all joy and excitement from our walk, leaving us with an outward veneer of Christianity. It is death to the Christian walk, for it makes the Christian walk harsh and demanding instead of exciting and joyous. Christ has set us free from the heavy yoke of legalism; let us not be bound again. Let us enjoy the freedom that God has given us.

Day 4: The Freedom to Flourish

> It is for freedom that Christ has set us free. Stand firm, then, and do not let yourselves be burdened again by a yoke of slavery.
> Galatians 5:1

Because legalism serves as such a great threat to our joy, we will continue to explore it today. We will delve deeper into what legalism means and what it means to walk by liberty (freedom in Christ).

How does Peter describe legalism in Acts 15:10?

_____

Challenge

What are the different yokes mentioned in Scripture? Match the verses with the correct yoke.

_____ Lamentations 1:14   A) Yoke of Christ

_____ Galatians 5:1   B) Yoke of Sin

_____ Matthew 11:28-30   C) Yoke of Slavery/Legalism

Which yoke are you currently wearing (be honest). If you are not wearing the yoke of Christ, what do you need to change in your life?

_____

Paul compares legalism to a yoke of slavery. In Old Testament times, a yoke was placed around the neck of oxen to bind them so they could pull a plough. As non-believers, we wore a yoke of sin (Lamentations 1:14); as legalists a yoke of bondage (Galatians 5:1), but as believers living free, we accept the yoke of Christ (Matthew 11:28-30).[4] In Matthew 11:28-30, Jesus promises us that his yoke is easy, his burden is light, and that we will find rest for our souls. At first glance, the last line seems a little paradoxical. How can a yoke be easy and a burden light? By definition, aren't yokes difficult and burdens heavy? This is the difference that Christ makes in our lives. His yoke is a personal relationship with him, and it is not wearisome because he loves us and seeks our best. He gives us rest from the exhaustion of continually following made up, rigid rules. It is not that we will not have challenges at times but that Christ enables us to bear them. His grace is always sufficient. The yoke of sin is enslaving, the yoke of legalism is oppressive, but the yoke of Christ is freeing.

Fill in the blank - John 8:36.

So if the Son sets you free, _____.

Exercise

Compare and contrast life under legalism with life under liberty (freedom in Christ). The first one has been done for you.

	Liberty (Freedom)	Legalism
Focused on externals or internals?	Internals	Externals
Depends on the flesh or Spirit?	_____	_____
Obeys because of love or obligation?	_____	_____
Produces humility or pride?	_____	_____
Results in bondage or freedom?	_____	_____
Causes us to move forward or backward in our Christian walk?	_____	_____
Results in joyfulness or joylessness?	_____	_____

Do you live legalistically or do you live freely in Christ? Place an X on the line below.

1 ——————————————————————— 10

Legalistic   Free in Christ

How are we to live (Galatians 3:11)?

_____

God's intended path in our Christian walk is liberty—freedom in Christ. "It is for freedom that Christ has set us free. Stand firm, then, and do not let yourselves be burdened again by a yoke of slavery" (Galatians 5:1). As Christians we have been set free—free from the penalty of sin and free from the power of sin in our lives

(Romans 8:2). But our freedom goes even deeper—it also means that we are free to love and please our LORD and him alone. Freedom allows us to become the people God desires us to be.

The life of liberty involves a walk of faith. "The righteous will live by faith" (Galatians 3:11). This verse is repeated four times in Scripture, underlying its importance (Habakkuk 2:4, Romans 1:17, Galatians 3:11, Hebrews 10:38). We live and walk by faith. In fact, "everything that does not come from faith is sin" (Romans 14:23). This contrasts with legalism which subtly transfers allegiance and trust in the LORD to a system of standards. Since legalism creates standards which meticulously define everything, one no longer has to exercise faith. But it takes more faith to pray, to listen for God's commands, and to wait patiently on him than to follow a meaningless series of *dos* and *do nots*.

Because legalism is works-centered, it also causes us to marginalize the LORD's standard which we could never meet. We create a replacement standard, one which we can easily fulfill, thus minimizing our complete need for the LORD. In Scripture, the Pharisees serve as a strong example of legalism. They created their own standards, adding countless rules to the Law. But we cannot formulize Christianity by creating an artificial set of rules.

What does Paul ask the Galatian Christians in Galatians 5:7?

_____

What challenges you most in your walk of liberty (freedom in Christ)?

_____

Read Galatians 5:16-18. How can we overcome legalism?

_____

How can we overcome legalism and live freely in Christ? Here are some general suggestions:

- *Maintain our relationship with God.* The heart of the Christian walk and the greatest deterrent to legalism is maintaining a living, vital relationship with the LORD. As we grow in our love for the LORD, our tendency to succumb to legalism diminishes.

- *Understand why we succumb to legalism.* We all succumb to legalism for different reasons. For instance, some of us succumb because we do not know better. It took me several years to realize that I had freedom in Christ and did not have to live under the harsh expectations of others. Or perhaps, we do not realize that God loves us unconditionally. We may create rules in an effort to earn God's love. Or maybe, we desire praise from others. Legalism provides the means to exalt ourselves above others. Or perhaps we have become comfortable in our bondage. Freedom can actually seem daunting at first, and so we prefer the security of known bondage to that of unknown freedom. As we better understand why we succumb to legalism, we can keep from falling into its snare.

- *Extend grace to others and stop judging them*—Legalism feeds on the self-righteous judgments of others. It assesses other people's spirituality based on their deeds. So we must learn to extend grace in the grey areas. Since we will discuss this area in more depth in our *Wearied by People* chapter, we will not delve further into it here.

- *Embrace uniqueness and individuality in others*—It was never God's intention that all his children look and act alike. We all have different personalities and temperaments. The body has variety and it is beautiful because it allows God to display his glory in different and unique ways. If we place legalistic rules on others, we hinder them from becoming who God has made them to be and their ability to bring him glory.

- *Live by the Holy Spirit.* The life of liberty relies on the Holy Spirit to provide guidance and direction in our Christian walk. In legalism, rather than depending on the Holy Spirit, one relies on himself and the flesh. In doing so, he weakens the Holy Spirit's moving in his life and in the lives of others because, in creating rules, he has left no room for others to act as they feel Spirit-led. All spontaneity and creativity are squelched. We cannot create rules for others in places where Scripture is silent, or we hinder the Holy Spirit's working. "Since we live by the Spirit, let us keep in step with the Spirit" (Galatians 5:25).

Throughout Galatians, Paul encourages the Galatian Christians and us to stand firm in our liberty. Legalism abounds, and legalists desire nothing more than to confine us to their mold. Because legalism grows slowly and subtly, it can easily creep into our lives if we do not diligently guard against it. None of us start out by saying that we desire to be a legalist. Yet if we are not careful, over time legalism may subtly infiltrate our thinking, and we may find ourselves ensnared by a rigid and demanding system of rules. We may find that we care more about rules than people and more about security than freedom. The challenge for us now that we have tasted freedom is to continue to live in our freedom and not succumb to the enticing snares of legalism. "So if the Son sets you free, you will be free indeed" (John 8:36).

Day 5: Seduced by Sin

> Restore to me the joy of your salvation and grant me a willing spirit, to sustain me.
>
> Psalm 51:12

This week we have focused on how to produce the fruit of joy in our lives—by naturally abiding in the LORD and obeying his commands. The main reason that we stop producing the fruit of joy is that we choose to sin. Sounds so simple, doesn't it? And yet sin has such a devastating effect on our relationship with the LORD that we must take it seriously. Sin removes us from the umbrella of God's fellowship; thus we no longer abide in him, and we lose access to joy. Make no mistake about it—sin will strip our joy every single time.

Read 2 Samuel 11:1-5 about David's loss of joy and fellowship with the LORD. What happens between David and Bathsheba?

_____

What warning do we receive about temptation from James 1:13-15?

_____

List the 3 areas in which you are most prone to succumb to temptation.

1. _____ 2. _____ 3. _____

What guards do you need to place in your life to keep you from sinning?

_____

Second Samuel 11 reveals the sad tale of David and Bathsheba. Here is David, a man after God's own heart, a man who has faithfully served God; yet now in a moment of weakness, he commits a terrible series of sins.

David has been in Jerusalem serving as King for about ten years. Spring has arrived, and kings often use this time of year to wage war. King David, however, chooses to remain in his palace while a battle rages around him against the Ammonites. This is his first mistake. As he wanders to the roof, he sees a beautiful woman named Bathsheba bathing. Instead of fleeing from the temptation immediately, David embraces it head on and calls for Bathsheba. A servant warns David that this is the *wife* of Uriah, but David pays no attention. That is his second mistake. Then he commits adultery with her.

David is the king. He has a standard to set for his people. He has his people's trust to preciously guard. But in his passion and lust, David forgets all this; he also forgets the LORD's gracious provision to him and commits a great sin. In that moment, David chooses to gratify a physical need rather than to enjoy an eternal satisfaction. He chooses the lesser and will suffer greatly for it.

It is so easy to succumb to temptation. After all, Satan packages it so well and appeals to the longings and desires he knows we have. "But each one is tempted when, by his own evil desire, he is dragged away and enticed" (James 1:14). In James 1:14, the Greek words translated *carried away* or *enticed* mean "to catch fish by bait or to hunt with snares."[5] It involves the idea of a hunter or fisherman baiting his trap to capture his prey. Not a pretty picture, is it? And yet this is precisely what Satan does. He secretively baits his trap for us and lies in wait, but the trap is not obvious. No animal would willingly step into a trap if he saw it. No, the animal steps into the trap because he has been enticed by the bait—it appears so appealing and attractive that it distracts his focus and lures him into an unsafe place. We must not underestimate Satan for he is a formidable foe. Somehow Satan was able to incite one-third of the angels to rebel against our LORD (Revelation 12:3-4). Imagine, these angels saw the beauty and magnificence of God and still chose to side with Satan and rebel. What do you think Satan can incite us to do if we do not cling to our LORD and remain submitted to him?

James 1:13-14 also reminds us that each one of us is tempted—none of us lie immune from Satan's clutches. And the bait Satan uses for each of us is different just as we are different individuals. What may tempt one person may not tempt someone else, and vice versa. We must remain wise and place guards in the areas in which we know we are prone to stumble. Remember sin happens progressively, starting with a simple, small desire that we entertain. King David, for example, always had a weakness for women. Though kings were not to have multiple wives, he adds wives as he seeks fit, ignoring God's initial command (Deuteronomy 17:17). Rather than placing a guard against his weakness, he entertains it and flirts with it. We must decide that we will no longer be seduced by sin for it carries a cost far too great for us. The LORD has promised us that when we are tempted, he will always provide a way out (1 Corinthians 10:13).

In addition to placing guards in our lives, it sometimes helps for us to consider the consequences of our sin, though Satan certainly tries to mask them. For example, if I am married and thinking about an affair, then instead of romanticizing the affair, I should consider the realistic effects of my choice - my spouse's devastation, my broken marriage, my children's distress, my broken fellowship with the LORD, and the loss of joy from my life. Considering the consequences can keep us from plunging headlong into the sin.

Read 2 Samuel 11:6-27. As a result of his adultery with Bathsheba, how else does David sin?

What does David lose because of his sin (Psalm 51:12)?
    ☐ God's love   ☐ His joy

Take a moment to reflect on your life. When you sin and lose fellowship with the LORD, do you experience joy or do you seem more irritable and unhappy?

After their adulterous night, Bathsheba conceives a child and alerts David to the predicament. Rather than repent and admit his sin, David attempts to cover it up by trying to get Uriah to sleep with Bathsheba. When this does not work, he kills Uriah. From a little adultery to murder, such is the nature of sin. A little sin soon ensnares us, and before we know it, we commit even greater sin.

After the announcement of Uriah's death, David waits for the mourning period to end and marries Bathsheba, acting as if he has committed no crime. From all appearances, David seems to have gotten away with his sin except for one small thing—he loses his fellowship with the LORD and the wondrous joy that comes with it.

Who confronts David about his sin (2 Samuel 12:1)?
  ☐ Nathan   ☐ Samuel

Read Proverbs 27:5-6. Do your close friends usually confront you when you sin or just sympathize with you? Explain.

Read 2 Samuel 12:1-15. Does God overlook David's sin? How does David's own sin come back to haunt him?

Allow the LORD to search and examine you. Do you have any unconfessed sin?

Months and months pass, Bathsheba gives birth to their child, and yet David does not repent. After patiently waiting for his repentance, the LORD finally sends the prophet Nathan to rebuke David. Nathan shares a parable of two men, a rich man who has many sheep and a poor man who has only one. The rich man, not content with his lot, seizes the sheep from the poor man. David becomes incensed at the rich man's treatment and demands to know who the rich man is. It is interesting, isn't it, that we easily see other's sins, but rarely recognize our own. David demands justice for the taking of a sheep, yet he has never repented for his taking of Uriah's life. Nathan then reveals that David is the rich man and that God has judged his sin. Do you notice that Nathan asks David, "Why did you *despise* the word of the LORD by doing what is evil in his eyes?" (2 Samuel 12:9a). When we sin, we choose to despise the Word of the LORD. Though time has passed, God has not forgotten innocent Uriah's death or David's terrible sin. David will not get by with his sin. "And you may be sure that your sin will find you out" (Numbers 32:23b). To David's credit, once Nathan confronts him, he immediately repents. He does not defend, rationalize, or deny his sin but rather accepts full responsibility (see Psalm 51).

Though God certainly forgives David, we cannot overlook the fact that David's sin is very costly; as the wages of sin usually are. Though God does not require David's life (an adulterer could be stoned), David's sin will still come back to haunt him. Before David's very eyes, one of his sons will lie with one of his wives. David will reap what he has sown (Galatians 6:7). But God's judgment does not end there. In the story Nathan shares with David, the rich man takes the poor man's sheep. Levitical Law required a fourfold restitution for the theft of a sheep (Exodus 22:1). Some scholars believe that David will have to repay four times Uriah's death. He will immediately lose the child born to Bathsheba, and in the years to follow, three of his sons, Amnon, Absalom, and Adonijah, will die violent deaths. David's sin will forever mar his name for even today, when Christians think of David, their minds immediately jump to this unsavory incident. This should serve as a strong warning to us. We cannot think that we lie immune from the consequences of our sin. We do not.

David also loses months of beautiful fellowship with the LORD and experiences months of joylessness. Unrepented sin in our lives will always result in empty, joyless lives. Sin is not something to be trifled with. It has serious consequences. I do not think David ever thought that committing adultery with Bathsheba would result in the death of Uriah, his loss of fellowship with the LORD, and his loss of joy. We cannot and must not underestimate the seductive temptations that come before us. Whenever we choose to sin, and we *choose* it, we are saying yes to a momentary satisfaction and no to lasting joy. We are choosing an earthly pleasure over an eternal fulfillment.

PART II:
The Joy-Stealers

Week 3:
Weighed Down by Worry

Day 1: The Weight of Worry

Day 2: The Battle for Belief

Day 3: A Loss of Focus

Day 4: A Perfect Peace

Day 5: Too Busy for Joy

Key Thoughts for the Week

Day 1:   Worry causes us to squander the blessings of today by keeping us focused on the possible problems of tomorrow.

Day 2:   Worry and belief are rivals in our heart, warring against each other for supremacy; when worry wins, belief loses.

Day 3:   One of the main reasons we worry is because we lose our focus, taking our eyes off the prize of Christ and losing ourselves in the problems of this world.

Day 4:   Through prayer, we release our burdens to the LORD and obtain the perfect peace of God, a peace that surpasses understanding.

Day 5:   We need to focus on God-ordained tasks instead of worldly focused activities, eternal pursuits rather than earthly diversions.

Day 1: The Weight of Worry

> An anxious heart weighs a man down.
>
> Proverbs 12:25a

Worry is one of the great thieves of our lives. It secretly steals our joy and pleasure, drawing us from the sweet embrace of our Father. It robs us of the happiness of today and the promise of tomorrow. Are you a worrier? Do you tend to obsess about certain things? Do you become overly anxious about the future? If so, this week should provide the extra encouragement you need to stop being weighed down by worry and to start trusting your all abundant and gracious Father.

Read Matthew 6:25-34 about worry and answer the following questions.

How many times does Jesus tell us not to worry?
☐ Two ☐ Three

What areas of worry does Jesus address? _____

Does worry help a problem?
☐ Yes ☐ No

Reflect on a recent instance in which you worried. Did worrying make the situation better or help you resolve it quicker? Explain.

_____

Who or what should we seek first at all times (Matthew 6:33)? Why?

_____

What is worry? Worry is the result of becoming overly concerned or apprehensive about something. It can start as a reasonable concern that turns awry because we unnecessarily fret over it. It often entails asking several what-if questions and then speculating on countless scenarios. The words translated *worry* or *anxious* come from a Greek word, *merimnao*, meaning "to be drawn in different directions."[1] And that is exactly what worry does. Our worries pull us one way while our trust in the LORD pulls us another way.

Worry can easily span the entire spectrum of our lives, if we allow it to. It can consume our time, energy, and thoughts. Knowing how easily we succumb to worry, Jesus commands us not to worry, reiterating his command three times in this short passage (Matthew 6:25, 31, 34).

In Matthew 6:25-34, Jesus addresses three main areas which may tempt us to worry: food, clothing, and the future. As Jesus addresses the area of food, he refers to the birds of the air. Most birds do not store away in barns, and yet the LORD feeds them. The LORD made the birds, and he takes care of them. This does not mean that the birds do not work diligently to secure food but rather that they do not worry about where their food will come from. We are far more valuable than the birds, for we are created in God's image; thus if God provides for the birds, he will provide for us.

In dealing with the second area of worry, clothing, Jesus talks about the lilies of the field. The lilies grow and do not worry about their coverings. Even King Solomon with all his riches and dressed in all his splendor was not as beautiful as one of these lilies. If God provides for the lilies of the fields, which are here today and gone tomorrow, he will also provide for us.

Finally, Jesus discusses worry related to the future. In today's times, we seem especially prone to worry about our futures. We desire security and protection, but our security and protection are found in the LORD and not in the circumstances of this world. No one can predict what will happen tomorrow. "Man is like a breath; his days are like a fleeting shadow" (Psalm 144:4). We should not waste our time and energy worrying about tomorrow and adding unneeded worries to our life. Sometimes we think that we will be joyous tomorrow once our worries are gone and our problems have been resolved, but the worries of today are usually replaced with the worries of tomorrow. Let's instead learn to live one day at a time and to enjoy the beauty of that day, leaving our worries at the foot of the cross with our LORD.

Do you sometimes lose the joy of today because you are worried about tomorrow and its possible problems? Check the answer that best describes you.

    ☐ Frequently   ☐ Sometimes   ☐ Rarely

According to Philippians 4:19, what will God meet?

    And my God will meet _____ according to his _____ in Christ Jesus.

No matter the worry—whether it is health, work, money, children, marriage, parents, or insecurity over the future—God has promised to provide for those who love him. He promises to meet all of our needs, not some of our needs, not a few of our needs, but all of our needs. "And my God will meet all your needs according to his glorious riches in Christ Jesus" (Philippians 4:19). And most of the time, the LORD provides exceedingly more than what we could imagine. Please understand that this does not trivialize our problems. For some of us, putting food on the tables every night is a challenge. For others, it may involve satisfying the different demands on our time. Our problems are real, but God's provision is just as real.

What does an anxious heart do (Proverbs 12:25a)?

_____

Challenge

Read Matthew 13:1-9, 22. Why is the seed that falls among the thorns unproductive?

_____

Exercise

List everything that you are currently worrying about in the lines below.

_____   _____   _____

_____   _____   _____

_____   _____   _____

_____   _____   _____

Now imagine you are climbing a mountain and carrying a back pack. Each of these worries represents a ten-pound weight. How do you think these weights will affect your performance?

_____

So how do your worries hinder you *spiritually* in your Christian walk?

_____

As you climb the mountain and seek to reach the summit, can you imagine how much an extra forty pounds of weight would physically slow you down? A short trek could easily turn into a long marathon as you physically exhaust yourself and struggle under the burden of the heavy weight. Even the slightest bump now becomes a major obstacle because you are so weighed down. Let's continue our analogy and compare the worried traveler (holding perhaps forty pounds of weight) with a worry free traveler (holding no weight).

- The worry-free traveler enjoys nature, views the trail appreciatively, and absorbs the beauty of his path. He is also less likely to become injured because he is so aware of his surroundings. The worried traveler is too exhausted and under too much pain to enjoy anything. He can only focus on getting over the next ridge. He may also fall victim to snares that he never realized awaited him because he is so inwardly focused.

- The worry-free traveler can help other travelers who have fallen or become injured. The worried traveler is too tired and pre-occupied with his situation to assist others. He has exhausted himself on his own journey.

- Both travelers are on a journey, but one enjoys the beauty of the path and the experiences of the journey while the other is so focused on the struggle to complete the journey that he misses the beauty and joy around him.

Spiritually, our worries and stresses do the same thing. They weigh us down from experiencing joy in our LORD and distract us from reaching our true goal in this life. Proverbs 12:25a reminds us that "An anxious heart weighs a man down."

And what does worrying really accomplish anyway? Does it solve the problem? Does it help find an answer? No. In many instances, it creates stress and havoc, causing sleeplessness and sickness. Worry is emotionally, physically, and spiritually draining to us, robbing us of the joy of our Christian walk. In Matthew 6:27, Jesus profoundly asks, "Who of you by worrying can add a single hour to his life?" Worry does not add a single hour to this life. In fact, the opposite is true. Many times we lose countless hours consumed by our worry.

Most of what we worry about will probably never happen anyway. Imagine the countless hours we could waste on unnecessary anxiety. We could have instead used our time and our thoughts to focus on the LORD and our relationship with him. Worry is one of Satan's greatest tools to keep us distracted from pursuing the LORD and eternal things. Think back, for instance, to when you were a teenager. Can you remember one of your worries? Does that worry matter today? How much time have we needlessly wasted on things that do not impact eternity?

In this life, there will always be things about which to worry. Life is challenging. We live in a fallen world, riddled with sin and its consequences. Events rarely occur as we envision them, and new issues always seem to surface. We cannot, however, succumb to worry. God has won the war and will provide for us as promised. We cannot squander the blessings of today by worrying about the possible problems of tomorrow.

Day 2—The Battle for Belief

> Commit your way to the LORD; trust in him.
>
> Psalm 37:5

Sometimes we worry because we do not truly believe God and his promises. Even though we may say that we believe God, in our hearts we do not really trust in his provision for us. Yet worry and belief are incompatible in our Christian walk. They are rivals in our heart, warring against each other for supremacy. When worry wins, belief loses.

How does worry demonstrate a lack of belief in God? Do we really trust God when we worry?

_____

What encouragement do you receive about trusting God from the following verses?

Psalm 37:5-6 _____

Isaiah 12:2 _____

When a problem arises, on whom do you normally depend?
☐ Family ☐ Co-workers ☐ Self
☐ Friends ☐ Neighbors ☐ God

Worry strikes at the very heart of our Christian walk. Why? Because one of the main parts of the Christian walk is to believe God. Worry demonstrates a lack of belief in our Father. We either do not believe in his power or we do not trust in his ability to solve our problem. Whether we realize it or not, worry is a sin. Non-believers worry because they do not believe that they have a Father who will provide for their needs. But we have such a Father, so why do we worry?

Sometimes, we may claim to believe in the LORD and to trust in his provisions, but our actions prove differently. Rather than trusting in our LORD, we trust instead in family members, friends, co-workers, neighbors, or oftentimes ourselves. We focus on our resources, strengths, and abilities. And yet our resources and abilities can often deceive us. We must not become wise in our own eyes. If we truly reflected on our limitations and weaknesses, we would never be tempted to trust in ourselves again. Why trust in our weaknesses and imperfections when we have God's strength and power? Instead, let's commit our ways to the Lord. "Commit your way to the Lord; trust in him and he will do this: he will make your righteousness shine like the dawn, the justice of your cause like the noonday sun" (Psalm 37:5-6). The Hebrew word meaning *commit*, *galal*, involves the idea of rolling; "one's ways and works [are] rolled onto (committed, entrusted) to someone (especially God)."[2] We need to roll off our problems onto the Lord. Only he can handle them. Only his back is strong enough to carry them.

Read Jeremiah 17:5-8 and compare the person who trusts in himself with the person who trusts in the Lord.

According to Proverbs 28:26, what are we if we trust in ourselves?
☐ Smart   ☐ Safe   ☐ Fools

Do you ever say you trust the Lord, but then think of a second option just in case the Lord does not come through? Is this really trusting in the Lord?

We also need to remove any false trusts from our lives and start trusting in the Lord *fully*. This means eliminating all "back pocket" options. Sometimes, we avow trust in the Lord, but we only trust him partially. We retain a small vestige of trust in the world or in ourselves. We keep that second option just in case the Lord fails to come through for us. And yet a partial trust is really no trust at all. George Muller was a man who whole-heartedly loved and served the Lord. During his life, he felt the Lord leading him to operate several orphanages to help impoverished children. Because Mr. and Mrs. Muller had sold their belongings and donated the money as alms to the poor, they possessed little money. Thus, he depended on the LORD *every day* to provide for the needs of the orphanage. There was no second option for Mr. Muller. If the LORD did not provide daily, then the children would go hungry. Some days, the table was even set for mealtime with no apparent food. And then from nowhere, someone would knock on the door and donate enough food to feed the children. Through all of it, Mr. Muller refused to worry or become anxious but always trusted God. And God was faithful. We do not need a second option, and we do not need to worry. God will always provide for us. It is ironic that we can sometimes trust the LORD with something as serious as our salvation, but then will not trust him with the daily problems of life, which are far less serious.

Our trust seems to decrease and our worry seems to increase significantly when the LORD fails to respond immediately to our situation. The longer we wait, the more we tend to worry. At these times, we may be prone to act impulsively, rushing into hasty decisions and moving ahead of God. Our lack of trust often gives way to worry, which tends to incite our impatience. Our impatience, in turn, causes us to make poor choices in an effort to resolve the problem quickly. So rather than experiencing God's best in a situation, we settle for the world's worst. Can you recall an instance in which you allowed your worry to cause you to act impulsively? No matter how long it takes for God to answer us, we must learn to wait for him. We must not rush into hasty decisions to appease our worry. Hasty decisions only cause greater worry and more anxiety in the long run and lead to a whole slew of new problems. "Do not fret—it leads only to evil" (Psalm 37:8b).

Sometimes it is not that we do not trust the LORD but rather that we fear his answer to our problem. Worrying often results from our desire to control circumstances and situations. We want to have lives our way, but our ways are rarely the best ways. Surely our past bruises and scars have taught us that we do not really know what is best for ourselves. Aren't we weary and tired of trying to control everything?

God's ways are perfect and his plans flawless. He always has the ideal solution for our situation, the perfect resource for our need. Let's stop trying to control that which we really have no control over. Did you notice that in Jeremiah 17:7-8, the person who trusts God is like a tree planted by the water? The tree does not fear when the heat comes; it does not worry when the drought comes. No matter what, it still bears fruit. Regardless of the circumstances plaguing it, it flourishes beautifully. Doesn't this sound enticing? Don't you want to be a tree that flourishes no matter the issues and problems of life? Peace, tranquility, rest, joy—no more stress, worry, and anxiety. This is what our LORD graciously offers us, if only we will believe him and trust him to provide. "Do not let your hearts be troubled. Trust in God; trust also in me [Jesus]" (John 14:1).

Read 2 Kings 19:32-36, which describes Assyria's planned invasion of Israel. How does God uniquely protect his people?

_____

Do you sometimes find yourself limiting God in situations and expecting him to behave a certain way? How can you be more open and trusting towards God's provision?

_____

Sometimes we struggle with fully trusting God because we forget the magnitude of God's power and his ability to meet our needs. Yet, Scripture tells us that God is omnipotent, meaning that God has all power. "Salvation and glory and power belong to our God" (Revelation 19:1). Because God is infinite, he possesses infinite power, power that knows no bounds. There are things God can do in his power that we cannot even imagine because our finite minds keep us from thinking in this dimension. If we could understand even the outer fringes of God's power and magnificence, we would never worry or fret.

As finite and limited creatures before an infinite God, we often expect God to behave in a manner consistent with our experience and learning. We tend to place him in our square box with little room for innovation. Yet God is infinite. He possesses infinite possibilities in working in a situation, and he rarely operates in the ways we envision. Since the LORD is omnipotent (possessing all power) and omniscient (possessing all knowledge), he has unlimited resources, power, and wisdom at his disposal. As problems arise in our life, they do not surprise our LORD or throw him off guard. He continually protects and cares for us, just as he did with the Israelites in 2 Kings 19. God is constantly working around us whether we perceive it or not, and he creatively comes up with solutions. We must leave room for him to surprise us. After all, who could envision that God would use a slingshot to kill a giant, a boy with five fish and two loaves to feed the multitudes, or an angel to slay 185,000 men?

What is there that God cannot do? What problem is so great that he does not have a solution? What issue is so enormous that he cannot solve it? God possesses an infinite number of possibilities, possibilities beyond our wildest imagination, to answer us. We should not worry or become discouraged because things do not seem to happen as we plan. Let us turn from our limited view to our LORD, knowing that he is unlimited and boundless. Lest us rest in his power, wisdom, and sufficiency. "Ah, Sovereign LORD, you have made the heavens and the earth by your great power and outstretched arm. Nothing is too hard for you" (Jeremiah 32:17).

Day 3: A Loss of Focus

> But my eyes are fixed on you, O Sovereign LORD; in you I take refuge—do not give me over to death.
>
> Psalm 141:8

One of the main reasons we worry is that we lose our focus. We take our eyes off the prize of Christ and lose ourselves in the problems of this world. This life is filled with challenges and difficulties. We cannot succumb to worry every time a problem occurs. We must keep perspective.

Read Matthew 14:22-28, which describes Peter's walking on water, and then answer the following questions.

Who places the disciples in the boat? _____

Describe the disciples during this episode. _____

Do the disciples recognize Jesus? ☐ Yes ☐ No

How does Jesus respond to the scared disciples? _____

Challenge

Is there anything that you currently fear and need to turn over to the LORD? What do Psalm 34:4 and Psalm 112:6-8 say about not being afraid?

_____

Does Jesus immediately help the disciples (Matthew 14:25)?
☐ Yes ☐ No

What does this tell you about how Jesus sometimes helps us in our lives?

_____

What does Peter ask Jesus (Matthew 14:28-29)?

_____

If you were in the boat, would you have asked Jesus this? Why or why not?

_____

After graciously ministering to the people, Jesus dismisses the crowds. Then, he sends his disciples ahead of him in a boat on the Sea of Galilee toward Capernaum. It is around 9 PM, and Jesus has retired to the mountainside where he can quietly commune with the Father. As evening approaches, a storm arises; strong winds start blowing, and the waters grow rough. The Sea of Galilee was known for such storms because cool air from the Mediterranean Sea often clashed with the hot air from the Sea of Galilee. At the fourth watch, a time between 3 and 6 AM, Jesus finally decides to join the disciples. Since the boat has traveled a great distance from shore, Jesus approaches them by walking on water. Isn't it encouraging that Jesus always meets us wherever we are and sometimes he uses extraordinary means?

Notice that it is the LORD who places the disciples into the boat, knowing of the impending storm. Sometimes the LORD allows storms in our lives to strengthen and mature us. The LORD also does not arrive as soon as the storm starts. He allows the disciples to spend several hours battling the storm before he appears. He could certainly have spared the disciples much anxiety and fatigue if he had come at an earlier time, but in his great wisdom and sovereignty, chooses not to do so. The LORD will always meet our needs, but he does not always come on our timetable.

Upon seeing Jesus, the disciples are terrified. At this point, they have been in their boat for many hours with much of the time spent battling the storm. They are probably tired and anxious. They are so focused on their situation that they fail to recognize Jesus. We can sometimes act in the same manner, can't we? We become so consumed with our problem that worry sets in and we fail to recognize the LORD as he comes to provide comfort. Jesus immediately calms their fears by revealing himself to them and telling them to take courage. He echoes the comforting words, "Do not be afraid." This is perhaps the most common encouragement that Scripture provides us. We are repeatedly encouraged not to be afraid.

Recognizing Jesus's great power, Peter asks the LORD if he will command him to come to him. Unlike in previous instances, Peter tempers his impulsiveness and first asks Jesus to command him. Then, amazingly, Peter walks on the water toward Jesus. Can you imagine the exhilaration of conquering nature and walking on water? What a thrill!

Continue reading Matthew 14:29-33 and answer the following questions.

What causes Peter to start sinking _____

How does Jesus respond to Peter? _____

What interesting thing happens when Jesus climbs into the boat? _____

What is the reaction of the people in the boat? _____

When you face a storm, what causes you to start sinking?

_____

On whom does the psalmist in Psalm 141:8 fix his eyes?

☐ Himself   ☐ His situation   ☐ the LORD

As the wind intensifies, Peter becomes afraid and caves to his fears. As he starts to sink, he desperately cries out to the LORD to save him. Jesus saves Peter but also rebukes him for doubting. As long as Peter focuses on the LORD, he is able to walk on water. But as he battles the elements, they distract his focus, and he begins to worry. As worry and fear rise in him, he begins to sink. It is easy for Peter to be distracted by the circumstances around him. The wind is blowing fiercely, and the waves are crashing. Peter goes from exhibiting great faith in one moment to life-threatening worry and distress in the next. Does that sound familiar? It is so easy to turn our eyes from our LORD to the circumstances of this world. We allow our career demands, health concerns, kid's welfare, daily food needs, clothing provisions, and the demands of our culture to shift our eyes from the LORD. It often begins as a subtle glance in which we begin to forsake time with our LORD to linger on the worries of the world. But the glances have a way of turning into stressful obsessions as we begin to focus our time and effort on "fixing" them ourselves or worrying about how they will turn out. As long as we remain focused on the LORD, the dismal circumstances and worries of this world will not affect us. "But my eyes are fixed on you, O Sovereign LORD; in you I take refuge—do not give me over to death" (Psalm 141:8). We need to take refuge in our LORD and place ourselves under his protection and security. As soon as we remove our focus, life will engulf us, and we will begin to succumb to worry and fear. But if we remain consumed by our worries and fear, we will miss all the exciting and exhilarating moments of this life because these moments require faith, not fear.

Before we judge Peter too harshly, we must give him credit. Of all the disciples in the boat, Peter is the only one to step out. He dares to ask and do the impossible. He risks it all. And what about us? When was the last time we stepped out on faith? When was the last time we risked it all and did the impossible?

Does Jesus allow Peter to sink (Matthew 14:31)?

_____

How does knowing that Jesus does not allow Peter to sink help you to step out on faith and to not worry?

_____

Let's end our homework today with one of Scripture's great encouragements. Fill in the blank – Luke 18:27.
What is _____ with men is _____ with God.

Jesus does not allow Peter to sink and drown, in spite of Peter's lack of faith. What a wonderful encouragement to all of us. The LORD will not allow us to sink either, even when we stumble and fall. After Jesus and Peter climb into the boat, the storm calms down. Jesus does not even command the wind to stop; it just miraculously stops when he climbs into the boat. In the LORD's presence, there is always calm for whatever storm we face. And, remember, sometimes the LORD calms the storm, and sometimes he calms us so that we can handle the storm.

Every day we battle against whether to believe God, and every day Satan tempts us to trust in ourselves and our resources. If we let him, Satan will distract us by keeping us focused on our problems and worrisome thoughts instead of on God and his power. We must learn to trust the LORD and to rest in his power and wisdom. We are royalty, children of the crown, surely we can trust our King to provide what we need. "Trust in the LORD forever, for the LORD, the LORD, is the Rock eternal" (Isaiah 26:4).

Day 4: A Perfect Peace

> Do not be anxious about anything, but in everything, by prayer and petition, with thanksgiving, present your requests to God. And the peace of God, which transcends all understanding, will guard your hearts and your minds in Christ Jesus.
>
> Philippians 4:6-7

As we discussed earlier this week, to overcome worry we must trust God and believe in his power to meet our needs. We must also bathe ourselves in prayer. Through prayer, we release our burdens to the LORD and obtain the perfect peace of God, a peace that surpasses understanding.

Read Philippians 4:5-7 about the importance of prayer and answer the following questions.

What should we pray about? _____

How should we offer our prayers? _____

How can prayer release us from worry?

_____

Do you take all your worries to the LORD through prayer? If not, do you get tired of having to daily bear your burdens? See Psalm 55:22.
☐ Constantly feel burdened   ☐ Sometimes feel burdened
☐ Rarely feel burdened

What encouragement do you receive from 1 Peter 5:7?

Cast all your anxiety on him because _____.

Ask the LORD to search you and write down any anxious thoughts you have. Now pray that the LORD would give you his peace.

In Philippians 4:6-7, Paul instructs believers to release their worries and anxieties to the LORD through prayer: "Do not be anxious about anything, but in everything, by prayer and petition, with thanksgiving, present your requests to God. And the peace of God, which transcends all understanding, will guard your hearts and your minds in Christ Jesus." Do you notice how Paul juxtaposes anxiety and prayer? They are mutually exclusive. If we are truly prayerful about something, then we do not remain anxious about it. And if we demonstrate anxiety, then we have not been truly prayerful.

Paul commands us to be anxious for nothing. So how many worries and cares does God permit us to have? Not one. Peter echoes Paul's thought as he instructs us to cast our cares on the LORD (1 Peter 5:7). This does not mean that we give the LORD a burden only to take it back five minutes later or a day later. We must once and for all give him our cares. Notice that Peter, like Paul, says that we must cast *all* our cares on the LORD. There are no problems too great and no issues too small that we should not lay them at the foot of the cross. Sometimes we feel silly seeking prayer for the little things of life, but God has concern for all the details of our life. In fact, insignificant cares can easily become significant problems if we do not release them to the LORD in the early stages. It is best to continually keep communication open with the LORD and to seek his direction, no matter how insignificant an issue may seem.

As soon as we feel anxiety creeping into our thoughts, we must stop our worrisome thoughts, pray about the issue, and trust the LORD for the result. The more we allow worrisome thoughts to enter our minds, the more those thoughts will build upon each other, growing and multiplying until we become totally consumed by them. As Paul writes to the Philippians, he could have easily surrendered to worry himself, for he is in prison awaiting a verdict on either his release or death. Instead, he encourages the Philippians and us to remain prayerful and to trust the Lord, as he himself is doing. Challenging situations provide opportunities for us to see God's glory revealed. It is exciting to anticipate how the Lord will work in a situation to meet our needs.

And do you notice how we should offer our prayers? With thanksgiving. Praise and thanksgiving enable us to see past the troubles of our circumstances and to focus instead on the goodness of our Lord.

Read Philippians 4:6-7 again. What guards our hearts and minds?

_____

How does Isaiah 26:3 describe God's peace for us?

_____

What comforting words does Jesus speak in the following verses?

John 14:27 _____

John 16:33 _____

How is God described in 2 Thessalonians 3:16?
☐ Lord of Prayer   ☐ Lord of Peace   ☐ Lord of Worry

Evaluate your *daily* level of peace by placing an X on the appropriate box below. If you are not experiencing God's peace daily, what do you need to change?
☐ Rarely at peace   ☐ Sometimes at peace   ☐ Always at peace

As we release our worries to the Lord through prayer, we receive the peace of God, a peace that surpasses understanding. The peace of God does not necessarily mean the absence of trouble or conflict but rather calmness during those times, an inner restfulness. The Greek word for peace *eirene* is similar to the Hebrew word *shalom* and refers to tranquillity regardless of people or circumstances, an inner calm. Such peace transcends our understanding and defies human logic. We cannot quite explain how, amidst a world of problems and hardships, we can possess tranquillity and calm. It is because we possess a supernatural peace.

The peace of God does not depend on our circumstances or the problems we face; it depends solely on our relationship with the LORD. Scripture describes the LORD as the God of Peace, *Yahweh Shalom* (Judges 6:24). Since we are now in Christ, we have access to God's abundant peace at all times as long as we remain in him. This is why in John 16:33, Jesus says that we *may* have peace. Peace depends on our remaining in our LORD. As soon as we stop abiding in Christ, we lose our peace. Notice in John 16:33 how Jesus contrasts peace *in me* with *in the world*. We can search for peace in the world. We can try to find it in money. We can seek it in our families. We can even pursue it in religious activity. But ultimately peace is found in only one person—our LORD.

In Philippians 4:6-7, Paul reminds us that God's peace guards our hearts and minds. The Greek word for *guard, phroureo,* is a military term involving a soldier standing guard.[3] Imagine a soldier pacing back and forth in front of his guard post, with weapon in hand, constantly on duty and aware of his surroundings. Similarly, God's peace stands guard around believers who trust him, keeping out anxiety and worry and covering those who rest in him. As long as we remain in fellowship with the LORD, we can experience his peace, a peace that surpasses understanding and that soothes our anxious spirits.

According to Philippians 4:8, what types of things should we think about?

Why is it important that we not only pray, but also redirect our worrisome thoughts?

_____

What should we do with what we have learned (Philippians 4:9)?

_____

To overcome worry, Paul does not simply tell us to pray, but he also instructs us to think about the right things (Philippians 4:6-9). Why? Because if we continue to focus on our anxious thoughts, we will never overcome worry. Our thoughts have a powerful impact on our actions and on our feelings. "For as he thinks within himself, so he is" (Proverbs 23:7, NASB). As soon as worrisome thoughts enter our minds, we need to stop dwelling on them and replace them with edifying thoughts; hence, the encouragement in Philippians 4:8 to dwell on whatever is pure, noble, right, pure, lovely admirable, excellent, and praiseworthy. This often takes an act of the will because if we allow even the smallest worrisome thought to enter our minds, we will become captive to them. Once drawn into its seductive cycle, one thought will lead to another, which leads to yet another. And before we know it, we will be down the well-worn path of worry. Another way to offset worrisome thoughts is to open our Bibles and start praying Scripture—this shifts our focus from the worrisome thoughts to positive, edifying thoughts.

Paul ends this section in Philippians by reminding us that we need to put into practice all that we have learned. Studying about worry and even memorizing the related verses will prove ineffective if, in the end, we will not practice what we have been taught. Life will always have its challenges. Yet God's promise to us is tranquility during the difficulties and peace in the storms. He stands as our protector, sustainer, and provider. We can release all our cares and burdens to him through prayer and allow his peace to guard and protect us. "Let the peace of Christ rule in your hearts, since as members of one body you were called to peace. And be thankful" (Colossians 3:15).

Day 5: Too Busy for Joy

> "Everything is permissible"—but not everything is beneficial. "Everything is permissible"—but not everything is constructive.
>
> 1 Corinthians 10:23

It would be hard to leave this week on worry without taking a moment to reflect on the busyness of our lives. One of the reasons we may worry and stress so much is the busyness and over-commitment of our schedules. Some of us tend to place too much on our plates and try to fit too much into our schedules. As a result, we can end up tired, wearied, and stressed. Let's spend a few minutes today trying to refocus on what is truly important.

Does our culture encourage busyness or slowness?

☐ Busyness   ☐ Slowness

Do you think culture impacts how you live your life?

_____

Read Luke 10:38-42. What prevents Martha from spending time with the LORD?

_____

Do you think that the LORD cares more about who you are or what you do? Is this reflected in the way you live?

_____

Spend a few moments with the LORD and honestly assess your schedule.

Is your schedule crammed with activities?

Do you do a quiet time everyday?

Do you have time to help others on the spur of the moment?

Would you describe your household as calm and relaxed?

Based on the above questions, do you think you need to slow down the pace of your life? If so, what changes do you need to make?

_____

The western culture in which we live tends to glorify busyness and the fast-paced lifestyle. Sometimes, our culture's view subtly infiltrates our thinking, and we believe that we need to have busy schedules filled with activities. While each of us is different, and some of us can certainly handle fuller schedules than others; all of us are at risk for over-committing. We must be careful to not pack our schedules with so many activities that we do not have cushion time. Otherwise, when problems occur, which they inevitably do, we become worried and stressed because we cannot meet the demands of our schedule.

So if we are too busy and over-committed, then what can we do? How can we simplify our lives? Let's explore a little further.

How do you determine your schedule for the day?

_____

What do you learn about Jesus's priorities from John 17:4?

_____

According to Psalm 90:17, who must establish the work we need to perform?

May the favor of the _____ rest upon us; establish the

_____ yes, _____.

Does God establish the work of your hands? As you add activities to your schedule, do you pray that these activities are God's will for your life or are you in the habit of just adding activities? Check the answer that best describes you.

☐ Always pray   ☐ Sometimes pray   ☐ Rarely pray

Exercise

Apply 1 Corinthians 10:23 to your life. Can you think of some activities in your life that are permissible, but not beneficial? Through prayer and the Holy Spirit, determine if you need to make any changes to your schedule.

I think we often expect too much of ourselves, demanding perfection in every area of our lives. As a result, we tend to place too much on our plates and over-schedule our time in an effort to accommodate everyone's needs and expectations. The result can be a frenzied pace of life. We may think that slowness is a luxury that we cannot afford, but quite the opposite is true. Slowness is a luxury we cannot afford *not* to have. Though our culture tells us that we can have it all, be it all, and do it all, we cannot. We cannot stay at the top of our careers, be wonderful spouses, be great parents, keep our households running, participate in every kid's activity, enjoy our hobbies, exercise daily, stay in touch with the cultural trends, be political activists, help in charitable activities, and remain active in our churches. It makes me tired just listing all those activities; I cannot imagine actually doing them. The result of our busyness and hectic schedules is often weariness, tiredness, and stress. We must learn to become more selective with the use of our time. Saying yes in one area frequently means saying no to other areas. Adding one more church commitment, for example, may mean less time with the family. Saying yes to one more hobby may mean saying no to a loved one. Though contrary to the dogma of our culture, there is nothing wrong with having open time in our schedule. We must prayerfully consider activities before we place them on our schedules, and if necessary, reprioritize some of our existing activities.

We also need to focus on performing only God-ordained tasks. Many times, we feel overwhelmed and stressed because we are not performing God-ordained tasks but rather an endless numbers of other activities, some of which have no eternal value. We unknowingly allow our personal agendas to distract us from God's true work. Or we try to accomplish both—we perform God's work but then also attempt to add other activities that are not in God's will for us. We must realize that we will never accomplish everything that this world offers. We must try to focus on that which has true eternal value. "Do not work for food that spoils, but for food that endures to eternal life, which the Son of Man will give you" (John 6:27). We cannot spend time doing all the peripheral activities of life and yet miss that which has the greatest significance. If we are too busy, for example, for a daily quiet time or prayer time, then we are simply too busy. Remember, the Lord is far more concerned with who we are than what we do. As we learn to focus on doing the Lord's will, we will experience more joyous lives rather than being constantly frazzled and stressed. This may, however, mean making some tough choices. We may have to reduce some of our activities or even some of our children's activities. Not all activities, though permissible, are beneficial for us. Some choices that seem to have a great earthly benefit may produce no eternal benefit; perhaps we need to forego some or all of these activities. Let's pray for spiritual wisdom and discernment to make choices that count for eternity.

It is interesting, that over the last few decades, technology has increased at a dramatic rate and enabled us to be far more efficient with our time than ever before. Today, we have inventions like washers, dryers, microwave ovens, cars, grocery stores, computers, and the Internet. And yet rather than allowing us to gain more freedom in our schedules, quite the opposite seems to have happened; our schedules are now sometimes busier than ever. Why? Perhaps because technology has created greater diversions in our life, thereby increasing our busyness. Television, hobbies, computer games, the Internet—diversions that can easily steal our attention. None are inherently bad, but we must place things in perspective. We cannot allow these distractions to create stress and worry in our lives. We cannot allow them to crowd out the excellent things. Technology and conveniences should enable us to grow closer to our Lord, not divert us away from him.

If we are not careful, the busyness and over-commitment of our schedules can cause us to miss the Lord and his wonderful presence. And then at the end of our lives, we will wonder why we did not witness his greatness and majesty more. Elizabeth Barrett Browning penned a beautiful poem that reminds us to take time and enjoy the Lord and the world around us.

> Earth's crammed with heaven
> And every common bush afire with God:
> But only he who sees, takes off his shoes,
> The rest sit round it and pluck blackberries,[4]

Let's slow down and cherish our time on this earth. Let's enjoy our Lord and our relationship with him. Let's focus on God-ordained tasks instead of worldly focused activities, eternal pursuits rather than earthly diversions. Over the thousands of years since creation, most things that have eternal value have never changed. Take a moment and really reflect on that. From the days of Adam and Eve until now, those things that have eternal value—the Lord and our relationship with him—have never really changed. As we place more and more on our schedules, we must make sure we are investing in the eternal and not the earthly. The eternal will always produce joy and peace in our lives.

Week 4:
Wearied by People

Day 1: The Royal Law

Day 2: The Difficulty of Differences

Day 3: The Hands of Compassion

Day 4: An Ambassador of Love

Day 5: The Peril of Pleasing Others

Key Thoughts for the Week

Day 1:   God has poured his love into us so that we can shower other people with the love we have received.

Day 2:   Much of the frustrations and irritations that we experience with people stem from differences in personality, dispositions, and traditions.

Day 3:   Demonstrating compassion often entails sacrifice and inconvenience.

Day 4:   Loving others deeply is our witness to an unbelieving world.

Day 5:   We must not try to please both man and God, or we may fail to truly please God.

Day 1: The Royal Law

> My command is this: Love each other as I have loved you.
>
> John 15:12

One of our greatest hindrances to joy often involves people. Though people should actually serve as one of our blessings, too often they end up being one of our burdens. It seems that people constantly irritate us, exasperate us, and drain us, all of which seems to strip the joy from our Christian walk. Though the world may be filled with irritable, cranky people, we cannot allow them to steal our joy. This week we will delve deeper into our personal relationships with one another, starting with an understanding of how the LORD commands us to treat others.

What are Jesus's two great commandments to Christians (Matthew 22:34-40)?

1. _____

2. _____

How does John 15:12-13 further echo Jesus's second commandment?

_____

Read Leviticus 19:18. Is loving others a new command?
☐ Yes   ☐ No

Fill in the blanks - Ephesians 5:1-2.
Be imitators of _____, therefore, as dearly loved children and live _____, just as _____ and _____ as a fragrant offering and sacrifice to God.

Exercise

For this week, we will focus on loving someone who seems hard to love. Spend a few moments in prayer and decide who this person will be.

As Jesus teaches, a Pharisee approaches him and asks a question. The Pharisees were the largest and most influential religious group during New Testament times, controlling both the synagogues and the common people. The Pharisees were known for zealously studying and keeping the Law. A Pharisee asks Jesus, "Which is the greatest commandment in the Law?" Jesus replies by saying that the greatest commandment is to love the LORD with all one's heart, soul, mind, and strength. Then, he adds the second commandment—to love one's neighbor as one's self. As Jesus responds to the Pharisee, he uses two commandments to summarize the entire Ten Commandments. Jesus's first commandment involves our relationship with the LORD and summarizes the first four Commandments, while his second commandment involves our relationship with others and summarizes the remaining six Commandments. Let's take a moment and truly reflect on what Jesus is saying. Loving others is second only to loving the LORD. If we were to perform two main acts in our Christian walk, it would be to love the LORD and to love others. As we reflect on what Jesus says, it begins to transform how we view others, doesn't it? We should not view people as a burden or an encumbrance, but rather as an opportunity and a blessing.

Loving others was not a new command for the Jews. Early in their history, the LORD stressed the importance of loving others. "Do not seek revenge or bear a grudge against one of your people, but love your neighbor as yourself. I am the LORD" (Leviticus 19:18). This command is frequently reiterated throughout the New Testament. "My command is this: Love each other as I have loved you. Greater love has no one than this, that he lay down his life for his friends" (John 15:12-13). As we speak of love, we must also understand that Jesus is talking about a selfless and sacrificial love, the type of love that places others before one's self. Jesus serves as the supreme example of such love for he died for us while we were sinners and his enemies.

Read 1 John 3:11-18 and 1 John 4:7-21 and answer the following questions about loving God and loving others.

From where does love come?_____

Do we know God if we do not love others?   ☐ Yes   ☐ No

How did God demonstrate his love to us? _____

According to Romans 5:5, what has God poured into our hearts?
☐ Truth   ☐ Love   ☐ Wrath

Why does the LORD stress the need for us to love others (Romans 13:8-10)?

_____

Challenge

Read 1 Corinthians 13:1-8 and answer the following questions about love. What do you learn about the importance of love? What should love do? What should love not do? Which attribute of love is the hardest for you?

_____

One of Scriptures most basic descriptions of God is that he is love. Since God now lives in us as Christians, he gives us his love to share with others. Listen to the way *The Message* describes 1 John 4:17-18: "God is love. When we take up permanent residence in a life of love, we live in God and God lives in us. This way, love has run of the house, becomes at home and matures in us." God encourages us to love others with the love he has provided us, but he also warns us that if we do not love others, we do not know him. "Dear Friends, let us love one another, for love comes from God. Everyone who loves has been born of God and knows God. Whoever does not love does not know God, because God is love" (1 John 4:7-8). These are challenging words, aren't they? We cannot claim to know God and yet not love others. Our love for others reveals the true depth of our love for the LORD.

First Corinthians 13, considered the love chapter of the Bible, stresses the importance of love in our lives. Though its main interpretation relates to spiritual gifts, it also reveals the different characteristics of love. As Paul addresses the Corinthian church, it struggles in the area of love, just as we may struggle today. Paul remarks that it is better to have love than the ability to speak in tongues, to posses the gift of prophecy, to have great knowledge, to have faith that can move mountains, or to give generously to the poor. Even if we die martyrs but do not possess love, we have *gained nothing*. That's amazing, isn't it? Without love, our actions remain hollow and empty. Love is the fulfillment of the law. It is the great tie that binds the rest of our virtues together, and it must serve at the heart of all we say and do. This places things in a slightly different perspective for us, doesn't it? Is loving others one of the great emphases in our lives? "Now that you have purified yourselves by obeying the truth so that you have sincere love for your brothers, love one another deeply, from the heart" (1 Peter 1:22).

First Corinthians 13 also reveals the various aspects of love. Love is patient, kind, and humble. It does not envy, boast, or keep a record of other's wrongs. It rejoices in truth. It protects, trusts, and hopes. Though the English translates most of the different aspects of love as adjectives, they are actually verbs in the Greek. Perhaps that serves as a good reminder to us that love is active, not passive. It is not something we talk about, it is something we do. Our love for others should be visible and tangible. Due to time constraints, we are not able to fully explore each different aspect of love, but I encourage you to spend time with the Lord and reflect on this passage. Apply it to your relationships with others. Are you demonstrating this type of love to others?

If we are honest, loving others does not come naturally to us. But God has poured out his love into us so that we can shower other people with the love we have received. Christians should serve as fountains that freely dispense God's love to others. Our love also serves as a great witness to this world. Though other people cannot visibly see God, they can see us loving them in tangible ways and reflecting God's love to them.

In the earlier set of questions, we primarily focused on the book of 1 John. Interestingly, 1 John was written by the apostle John, who is known as the apostle of love. If we were to study John, however, we would find that he was nicknamed "son of thunder" (Mark 3:17) because he wanted to call down fire on a village that refused to accept Jesus (Luke 9:54). Not quite the picture of love that we would expect. And yet our Lord completely transformed him so that he would become known as the apostle of love. Can you imagine the transformation? That is the transformation that Christ makes in all of us. Every day he transforms our thoughts and actions to reflect him. Every day we love him more and those around us more.

If you are like me, God's call to unconditionally love and accept others may seem overwhelming. But the Lord does not ask us to do this in our strength and power. We could not—we would fail miserably. The Lord will provide the grace we need, even to love those difficult people. We need to rest in him and allow him to work through us.

In this life, few things endure into eternity. The love we express for others is one of them. Ephesians 5:1-2 encourages us to live lives of love. We will spend all this life and all of eternity living in love because love is God's very nature. Remember the well-worn adage *"When you come to the end of your life on earth, it will not matter how long you have lived but rather how deeply you have loved."*

Day 2: The Difficulty of Differences

> Accept one another, then, just as Christ accepted you,
> in order to bring praise to God.
>
> Romans 15:7

In this world, we will always meet people who will challenge, irritate, and frustrate us. Much of this frustration, however, could be avoided if we realized that our personality differences, preferences, and traditions often create unnecessary problems and issues. Satan then uses these differences to cause division and friction within the body of Christ.

How can personality differences cause conflicts within the body of Christ?

_____

Read Romans 15:5-7. How should we treat others who differ from us? Why?

_____

Exercise

Is the person you selected on Day 1 difficult to love because of personality differences? Pray that the LORD will reveal a new truth to you about this person.

The underlying cause of much of the frustration and tension that we experience with other people stems from differences in personality, dispositions, and tradition. The LORD has hand crafted us as unique individuals with certain strengths and preferences. We also have our own weaknesses and annoying habits. God has made each of us beautiful in our own right but very different from one another, enabling us to use our individuality to bring him glory.

Our varied personalities cause us to view situations very differently. Each of us naturally evaluates a situation through our own prism, a prism that includes our predispositions, our personalities, and even our own sinful tendencies. Our prisms impact how we perceive events and normally include unwritten rulebooks in which we place expectations on people and circumstances, expecting people to react in a certain way for a given situation. For example, if we are sick, we may expect someone to call or bring us food. We normally expect people to react in a manner consistent with how we would react. But different people view situations from different perspectives. An elephant from the front looks quite different than an elephant from the back. We will not all see everything the same way, and we must not try to make everyone see things exactly like us, or we strip others of their individuality. We cannot prize uniformity over uniqueness. We will dishearten and discourage the body of Christ from fulfilling its God-ordained mission if we expect everyone to behave like us. For example, if Jennifer possesses the spiritual gift of mercy, she may find Michelle who has the gift of administration to be callous or unmerciful because Michelle seems more concerned with numbers than people. Michelle, on the other hand, may find Jennifer impractical and unrealistic. God has handcrafted both of these individuals but created them very differently. He has endowed each of them with different gifts because each serves a different purpose in bringing him glory. Ultimately, the body of Christ needs the strengths of both these individuals because they balance each other and allow the body as a whole to bring glory to God.

Read Acts 15:36-41 and answer the following questions.

About what do Paul and Barnabas disagree? _____

What is Paul's position? _____

What is Barnabas's position? _____

Why might Barnabas have held this position (Colossians 4:10, Acts 4:36)? _____

With whom do you tend to side?   ☐ Paul   ☐ Barnabas

Honestly assess yourself. Are you accepting of Christians who differ from you or who hold different opinions than you do?

_____

If we are honest, we sometimes struggle with accepting others who possess different opinions than us. And yet we have to learn to disagree graciously. Too often we are offended by those who hold a different opinion than ours. We may even think we are godlier because of the opinions we possess or the decisions we make. We forget that each area of disagreement usually has two sides and each side normally has some valid points. Remember that as we speak of accepting others' positions, we are discussing the grey areas, not the black and whites of Scripture. We are never to compromise on God's truths, like abortion, adultery, stealing, and so forth.

Acts 15:36-41 provides a great example of how two godly men, Paul and Barnabas, can disagree. The Greek word for *disagreement*, *paroxusmos*, means "the stirring up of anger, sharp contention, angry dispute."[1] Paul's and Barnabas's disagreement is not a mild difference but a sharp contention between two godly men. Initially, John Mark had served with these men on a missionary journey but then deserted them in Pamphylia and returned to Jerusalem. Now as the men discuss a second missionary journey, Barnabas favors taking John Mark who is his cousin, while Paul opposes it. Who is right? As we view this scenario, we will probably side with the person who best mirrors our personality. Barnabas is the epitome of compassion, a man gifted in encouragement. The early church affectionately referred to him as "son of encouragement" (Acts 4:36). Barnabas views the situation as a way to encourage John Mark. Paul, on the other hand, is a man of strong conviction and determination. He probably thinks that they should take someone more reliable on the mission. It is easy to understand both points of view, isn't it?

As we study this situation, we realize that Godly men, men devoted to the LORD, can and do disagree. In order to edify the body, we must learn to disagree graciously and to accept different opinions. Remember too that God could have used both opinions to work out spiritual consequences we cannot see. Perhaps taking Mark on Paul's journey would have been disastrous for Mark, as he may have faced things for which God knew he was not ready. And perhaps God also knew that Mark needed Paul's strong rebuke in order to deal with his previous desertion and weakness. At the same time, God may not have wanted Mark completely discouraged and so used Barnabas to show him mercy and mentor him. This would enable Mark to overcome his fears and to strengthen his resolve. In the end, God's kingdom will grow, and God will use four rather than two missionaries. And John Mark will redeem himself, for he will eventually write the Gospel of Mark.

Read Romans 14:1-13. Who should we accept? Check all that apply.
☐ The stronger brother ☐ The weaker brother ☐ Other Christians

Should we judge another Christian in grey areas of Scripture, like drinking alcohol or watching television (Romans 14:3-4, 10-13)? Explain.

_____

What additional guidance do we receive on judging others from Matthew 7:1-5?

_____

We do not need to create unity in the body of Christ—the LORD has already done that. We only need to preserve such unity by accepting and loving our brothers and sisters and not passing judgment on them in grey areas of Scripture. The Greek word for *accept* in Romans 15:7 means "to receive to oneself, admit to one's society and fellowship, receive and treat with kindness."[2] We need to receive those who differ from us into our groups and treat them with kindness. In Romans 14, Paul provides an example of two believers; one believer thinks it is acceptable to eat everything, and the other does not. The believer who eats meat should not condemn the believer who does not, and the believer who eats only vegetables should not judge the believer who eats meat. Why? God has accepted both men because both men are living by faith. Within the Christian walk, there are many grey areas, areas in which Scripture neither affirms nor denies a particular position but where the LORD has given individual conviction. In these instances, we must rely on the Holy Spirit to provide the guidance we need and must not judge the choices of another Christian.

Scripture repeatedly warns Christians against judging others self-righteously or hypocritically. "Stop judging by mere appearances, and make a right judgment" (John 7:24). Why does Scripture command us to not judge others self-righteously? There are many reasons, but here are a few: we do not possess full information, we cannot discern motives, we judge based on our predispositions. We also tend to judge others using our strengths but their weaknesses.

Please notice that Scripture does not say that we should never judge another person but rather that we should not judge him self-righteously. Judgment is a necessary element in the body of Christ. We must discern false teachers, the LORD's truth for our lives, sound Christian advice, our own sin, others sin for the purpose of restoration, and so forth. The LORD does not, however, reveal another person's sins and weaknesses to us so that we can self-righteously judge them but rather that we might pray for them and help them in their walk.

We are also wise to remember that we are all at different stages in our Christian walk. The LORD does not conform us over night; sanctification is a long road. We may be more mature than someone else; thus certain aspects may come easier for us. We should not condemn but disciple out of love. We sometimes forget that it is by the grace of God that we are who we are and where we are; for it is the Holy Spirit who every day conforms us to the image of Christ and gives us victory over sin.

We provide Satan a great foothold when we do not accept and love our brothers and sisters in Christ. We must not naively believe that Satan only uses non-Christians to attack God's work and God's people. Satan tries to use Christians, and he frequently prevails because we succumb to his snares. We must learn to accept each other with all our faults, problems, and blemishes, remembering the LORD's great acceptance of us. "Accept one another, then, just as Christ accepted you, in order to bring praise to God" (Romans 15:7).

Day 3: The Hands of Compassion

> Therefore, as God's chosen people, holy and dearly loved, clothe yourselves with compassion, kindness, humility, gentleness and patience.
>
> Colossians 3:12

Today we have the privilege of studying about compassion through the eyes of Jesus. In Matthew 14, we find Jesus feeding five thousand men. This is the only miracle recorded in all four of the gospels and provides us wonderful insight into loving and serving others.

Read Matthew 14:13-21 and answer the following questions.

Why does Jesus retreat to a solitary place (Matthew 14:9-13)?

_____

Describe Jesus's emotions for the crowds. _____

What do the disciples ask Jesus to do in Matthew 14:15?

_____

Is the disciples' request practical? ☐ Yes ☐ No

Has practicality ever inhibited you from expressing compassion to someone? Explain.

_____

As God's people, with what should we clothe ourselves (Colossians 3:12)?

_____

The crowds follow Jesus as he travels from place to place. Some follow to hear his teaching, others to see his miracles. Still others pursue him because they believe he will usher in the Messianic kingdom and overthrow the Roman reign. In Matthew 14, the crowds follow Jesus to the Sea of Galilee, a small lake about thirteen miles long and eight miles wide. It is close to the Jewish Passover time, a time in which the Jews paid homage to God for their great deliverance from Egypt. Jesus retreats to a mountain to be alone because Herod has beheaded John the Baptist, his friend and cousin. He also retreats for security reasons to avoid capture by Herod, for his time had not yet come. Jesus desires quiet and solitude.

Though Jesus desires quiet, the crowds follow him and allow him no rest. Jesus's response to them is remarkable. He demonstrates great compassion and kindness. Rather than telling the people to leave, he cares for them. He heals the sick. He teaches the masses. Though tired and probably weary himself, he selflessly serves them, placing aside his own personal needs. The Merriam-Webster Dictionary defines compassion as "sympathetic consciousness of others' distress together with a desire to alleviate it."[3] Compassion often involves empathy, in which we place ourselves in someone else's shoes. The Greek word for *compassion* actually involves being moved in the bowels. [4] The Greeks considered the heart of their emotions to reside in their intestinal areas. Thus, compassion refers to the strongest of emotions. It is a heartfelt desire to help others. Jesus's compassion is overwhelming. Take a moment to truly reflect on it. Jesus has recently experienced the death of John the Baptist. He craves solitude and time for reflection, yet he puts aside his personal needs to minister to the crowds who follow him. If ever he could justify a lack of compassion, it would be now. This is a time where he needed to receive compassion from others, not give it out. Yet he still manages to extend compassion and to help the crowds.

And do you notice that Jesus serves them until late afternoon? Jesus does not give only one or two hours of his time to placate them, he selflessly serves them for hours. How would we have reacted if we were Jesus? Would we have been irritated and perhaps even resentful to have people demanding our attention and needing our assistance when we craved solitude? Extending compassion to others often means placing other's needs before our own. It seeks their good, even at personal cost.

Weary and tired, the disciples need a time to rest and to reenergize themselves. Mark 6:30-32 elaborates that they have not even had the opportunity to eat. Serving with Jesus all day probably exhausts them even more. By evening, they tell Jesus to dismiss the crowds so that the people can go into town to buy food. After all, five thousand men probably means more like ten to fifteen thousand total people including women and children. The prospect of feeding all these people would prove a sizable and expensive task. In asking Jesus to dismiss the crowds, the disciples act practically (please notice that the disciples had enough compassion to want the crowds to be fed), but they forget that before them stands the great provider, that with God nothing is impossible. Instead of asking him to find a way to feed the people, they choose the practical way out. But practicality and common sense can sometimes become stumbling blocks if we use them to rationalize away someone else's need. They can also prevent us from seeking the abundant provision of the LORD.

How does Jesus respond to the disciples' request (Matthew 14:16-21)?

_____

How many basket(s) of food are leftover (Matthew 14:20)? What does this tell you about God's provision?
- ☐ 1 basket   ☐ 5 baskets   ☐ 12 baskets

Fill in the blank - James 4:17.
    Anyone who knows the good he ought to do and doesn't do it

_____.

Read 1 John 3:18. When was the last time your compassion caused you to re-arrange your schedule to meet the need of another? Explain.

_____

Exercise

Think of a tangible way in which you can demonstrate compassion to the person you selected on Day 1.

Jesus refuses to dismiss the crowds without feeding them. He knows the crowds are tired and hungry, and he will not send them away empty. Throughout Jesus's ministry, he always demonstrates compassion for other people. He frequently takes time to help others, healing the blind, curing the lepers, and restoring the sick to health. As Jesus surveys the crowds, he knows the crowds are fickle and will soon turn from him, yet he offers compassion to them anyway.

    Compassion is also active, not passive. John reminds us that we must not love with only words or tongue but with actions and in truth (1 John 3:18). Love is visible and proactive. It does not only offer to pray for someone, as commendable as that is, without taking the effort to actually help them (if that is possible). We must also remember that as we compassionately help others, we may not always receive the thanks or reward that we should. Some people may seem ungrateful or even critical of our assistance.

Demonstrating compassion to others does not always fit into our predetermined schedules. Many times, it causes inconvenience. What type of attitude do we express when someone needs assistance? Do we resent the intrusion on our time, or do we allow the Holy Spirit to guide us? Sometimes we forget that this life is not about us or our plans but about God and his plans. Let's ask God to help us to surrender our time and our plans to him.

In the end, Andrew brings a little boy who has five small barley loaves and two small fish to Jesus. Jesus then uses this little boy to perform a miracle and feed almost fifteen thousand people. As the disciples collect the remnants of leftover food, they realize that it fills twelve baskets. What the LORD does, he does in abundance, exceedingly more than all we could ask or imagine (Ephesians 3:20). Whenever we demonstrate compassion to help others, the LORD will intervene and help us if we need it. If he can use a boy's lunch to feed the multitudes, imagine what can he do with our resources?

As we close today, some questions may naturally arise. When we deal with challenging people, can we place boundaries? Can we subtly extract ourselves from interactions with them? These are honest but difficult questions. First, we must seek Godly wisdom for our answers. We need to pray and ask the LORD for counsel. Second, we must look to the example of Jesus. Did he place boundaries on his compassion to others? Did he turn people away because he had helped them repeatedly and they still seemed to drain him? Jesus often expended and exhausted himself for people. Most people probably drained and depleted him, yet Jesus continued to offer them assistance. This may incline us to believe that we should meet every need. But Jesus did not meet every need he saw. And we cannot meet every need we see, and the LORD has not meant for us to. Sometimes we may need to graciously say no. How can we know when to say yes and when to say no? We must listen to the Holy Spirit—this is the third step. Each of us has the Holy Spirit within us, and God is more than able to guide us to what he wants us to do. Sometimes our emotions tell us that we have done enough and that we do not deserve such treatment, yet God may choose for us to continue to minister to people and to show them the love of Christ. At other times, the Holy Spirit may tell us to walk away. The Holy Spirit and not our emotions should serve as our guide.

We live in a world desperately in need of compassion. We need only open our eyes. Sometimes we become so inwardly focused that we fail to see the hurting people around us crying out for help. Let's try to remain sensitive to the Holy Spirit and allow him to guide us. Perhaps we need to pray for more sensitive hearts as our hearts tend to harden over time, especially when someone has taken advantage of us. We are the hands of Christ. We are his feet. "Therefore, as God's chosen people, holy and dearly loved, clothe yourselves with compassion" (Colossians 3:12a).

Day 4: An Ambassador of Love

> But I tell you: Love your enemies and pray for those who persecute you.
>
> Matthew 5:44

One of the most remarkable aspects of our LORD's love for people was that it was unconditional. It did not depend on who they were, what they possessed, or how righteously they acted. He interacted with sinners as much as priests, the rich as much as the poor, the healthy as much as the sick. He always demonstrated unconditional love, loving people just as they were. And he loved not only his friends, but acquaintances, difficult people, and even his enemies. As we complete today's lesson, I will warn you that Jesus spoke many challenging words to us concerning our *unconditional* love of others. Allow the Holy Spirit to serve as your guide as you study some of his words.

Read Luke 14:12-14. When we host a luncheon or dinner, who do we normally invite? Who does Jesus want us to invite?

_____

What does Romans 12:16 tell us?

_____

How well do you show love to those who are not your friends and family members? Honestly evaluate yourself using the following scale and place an X.

1 ———————————————————————— 10

Love friends and family   Love outcasts

In Luke 14:12-14, Jesus provides rich advice on how to demonstrate our love to others. He says that when we host a luncheon or dinner, we should not invite only our friends and family but also the poor, the crippled, and the blind. Jesus's society considered these people outcasts, and thus they did not receive invitations to banquets and social events. Jesus speaks against the common custom of entertaining people who entertain you. We tend to reciprocate kindness with more kindness. Jesus, however, says we receive no reward when we invite our friends and family members because they will repay our generosity by inviting us back. It is instead when we invite the outcasts and the misfits, that the LORD will bless us because they cannot repay our kindness.

If we are honest, most of us do a fairly good job of showing love to our friends and family members. It is easy to be nice to those who are nice to us, but unconditional love is shown to all people. How well do we do with acquaintances and outcasts? Years ago, my husband and I were involved in a married couples' Bible study class in which I had the opportunity to attend the baby shower for two different women in our class. One woman, whom I will call Mary, was a sweetheart, kind and caring. She was liked by all. She had over thirty ladies from our class attend her shower. The other lady, whom I will call Janice, was very different. Life had been hard on her, and her personality and demeanor showed it. Though a beautiful woman in Christ, her exterior and her actions were abrasive. Only one lady from our class attended her shower, and Janice was understandably hurt. What seems most surprising about this story is that it occurred in our church Bible study class. Though we certainly cannot help everyone because we are time constrained, we must look deep into our hearts and honestly assess if we are advancing the LORD's kingdom or our own comfortable worlds. It has well been said that those who need love the most often receive it the least. So let's ask the LORD to open our eyes to the hurting people around us and to give us a heart that aches for them.

Though Jesus commands us to love others, he is not saying that we should live lives devoid of friendships and that we should never entertain our friends. Christian friendships are one of God's most precious gifts to us, but they must be balanced and kept in perspective of our whole Christian walk. We have all of eternity to develop relationships with our friends, but we have only a very limited time to share the love of Christ with others, especially non-believers. Once we arrive in heaven, it will be too late.

Read Matthew 5:38-47. How should we treat our enemies?

_____

According to Matthew 5:46-47, if we only love those who love us, we are no better than a _____.

Have you ever had to love an enemy? What did God teach you?

_____

Reclaiming Your Joy

In Matthew 5:43-47, Jesus makes some pretty shocking statements. He completely raises the bar for the treatment of one's enemies. Rather than responding with hate for an enemy, Jesus commands Christians to love those who hurt them. Much of our love frequently involves a self-serving element. We love those who love us. We help those who help us. Jesus, however, wants us to love selflessly—with no ulterior motive and with no strings attached—to love those who will not always return our love, to help those who cannot help us back. In Matthew 5:38-42, Jesus further explains his idea of love by providing several examples of expected behavior:

- First, Jesus commands us to turn the other cheek when someone slaps us. The Jews considered a slap on one's cheek a great affront. It insulted the person's honor and dignity. Jesus stresses that rather than retaliate, we should give the person our other cheek—in essence, act humbly and do not avenge the wrong committed against us. Let me also clarify that Jesus does not mean for us not to defend ourselves during times of war, not to respond in self-defense when facing bodily threat, or to remain in abusive relationships, he means for us to not pursue vengeance against others.

- Second, Jesus says if anyone tries to take our shirt, we should also give the coat. The shirt referred to a long tunic or inner garment, normally made of linen. It was more of an undergarment, while the coat was considered an outer garment. The Mosaic Law commanded the return of a person's coat before sundown (Exodus 22:26-27). The immediate context of this verse involves legal proceedings in which someone has sued us. If the court found us liable, then we should give our shirts as payment of the debt. Jesus commands us to go further and to also provide the coat if the coat will fully repay the amount owed. Because of the Law, the court could not demand the coat, but the person could willingly surrender it to make amends.

- Third, Jesus says that whenever someone forces us to go one mile with him, we should offer to go two. Roman law allowed a soldier to force a civilian to carry his gear for one mile. Though soldiers viewed this as a great benefit, civilians possessed a great aversion to it. Being forced to abandon one's existing duties to carry a soldier's heavy equipment was an insult. Not only did one have to delay his existing plans, but he was forced to assist his oppressor. Jesus challenges us to not only provide the required but to also give the unexpected and to do so with a cheerful disposition.

- Fourth, Jesus commands us to give to whoever asks and not turn away from the one who wants to borrow from us. In this directive, Jesus wants us to surrender our rights for material possessions. He wants us see others as more important than ourselves and to help those genuinely in need of assistance.

The heart of Jesus's teaching involves our willingness to surrender our rights in order to reveal Christ to the unsaved and to help mature our brothers and sisters. Paul repeatedly surrendered his rights in order to promote the gospel with others. We too must set aside our rights in order to promote the gospel and to magnify God to the world. Remembering how we acted as enemies toward our LORD before our salvation and his loving response to us may enable us to act mercifully and lovingly toward others.

Read Matthew 5:44. How can praying for our enemies or for a difficult person help?

Exercise

Commit to pray daily for the person you selected on Day 1 and for your relationship.

Jesus also calls us to pray for our enemies. Why? Praying cleanses us from ill will toward others. It is difficult to pray for someone and at the same time to harbor hatred and resentment against them. It also makes us an active participant in seeking other people's betterment and reconciliation with God. Slowly God will reveal the positive aspects of their personality instead of us magnifying their weaknesses. As a result, it makes it much more difficult for us to retain a grudge against them.

When we encounter a difficult person or an enemy, we may think that if we could remove this one person from our life, we would be more joyous. But people should not determine our joy, and they should not steal our joy if the source of our joy is truly the LORD. In fact, the LORD often uses other people to reveal our imperfections and sins. Someone once compared our enemies to sandpaper. The LORD uses them to smooth out our rough edges. He uses them to grow and mature us. He intentionally allows circumstances so that we are forced to learn to love others deeply and not superficially.

We must commit to loving people, regardless of how difficult they may be. What if one of our main tasks in this life is to love and minister to that difficult person whom we would rather avoid? As Christians, love is our witness to an unbelieving world. We show the incredible, abundant love we have received by showering it on those around us. And yet loving others, especially our enemies, is not an easy task. But our LORD does not ask us to accomplish it in our strength. He asks us to trust him and to allow him to live through us. He will give us the grace and strength we need to forgive those who hurt us and to love those who demean us.

Day 5: The Peril of Pleasing Others

> Am I now trying to win the approval of men, or of God? Or
> am I trying to please men? If I were still trying to please men,
> I would not be a servant of Christ.
>
> Galatians 1:10

When it comes to people, we seem to veer in one of two directions.
Either we focus too much on ourselves, failing to extend compassion or love to others, or we seek to please others at the expense of
pleasing our LORD. Both extremes are wrong. Since we discussed the
former in the earlier part of the week, today we will discuss the latter.

List some people you seek to please.

_____

Read 1 Thessalonians 2:1-6 and answer the following questions.

Who is Paul trying to please? _____

Who is Paul not trying to please? _____

How does Galatians 1:10 further echo Paul's desire?

_____

Reflect on your life. Who do you seek to please *most*? Check the
appropriate answer.

☐ God   ☐ Myself   ☐ Others

How can seeking to please people hinder our Christian walk?

_____

Embedded within many of us is the desire to please others. We want others to like us. We want them to think nice thoughts about us. In Galatians 1:10, Paul says, "Am I now trying to win the approval of men, or of God? Or am I trying to please men? If I were still trying to please men, I would not be a servant of Christ." Paul was initially a people pleaser. Does that surprise you? Yet, Paul asked if he were *still* trying to please men? There was a time in his life when Paul tried to please the religious people, but the Lord was able to help him refocus on only pleasing the Lord. That should serve as a wonderful encouragement to us. Sometimes we place Paul on a pedestal, forgetting that it is the Lord's grace and strength that worked through him; and that same grace and strength is available to us.

The Greek word *aresko*, translated *please*, means "to seek to please or gratify, to accommodate oneself to."[5] When we please others, we accommodate ourselves to them. We conform to their standards and desires in order to win their approval of us. Whether we realize it or not, it is very difficult to please both man and God. Someone will usually lose, and many times it is our Lord. Though we may certainly try to please people at times in order to make the gospel more accessible, we are never to do so at the expense of pleasing the Lord. There is a great cost to pay for the desire to please men—the main one being our relationship with the Lord. Whenever we decide to place someone or something before the Lord, it never has a favorable result.

According to 1 Corinthians 7:23, what should we not become since we have been bought by the precious blood of our Savior?

☐ Slaves to God ☐ Slaves of men ☐ Slaves to ourselves

Are we truly free if we seek to please others or have we become slaves of men?

What will the fear of man prove to be (Proverbs 29:25a)?

_____

The desire to please others places an inordinate burden on our self-esteems. As a result, our esteems may become linked to other people's acceptance of us or their opinions. As others dislike what we say or do, it may severely damage our self-confidences. There will be times when others think the worst of us; they will misunderstand our actions or misconstrue our intent. It is an overwhelming feeling to be at the mercy of another person's opinion.

The desire to please others also hinders the will of God in our lives, for we become consumed with what others will think of us. If we do not believe that others will view God's directives favorably, then we may fail to perform them. For instance, we have a friend whom the LORD called to leave her profession as a doctor in order to become a missionary and to home school her children. Had she sought to please others, she would not have left a lucrative, prestigious career in order to home school her children. Proverbs 29:25 reminds us, "the fear of human opinion disables; trusting in God protects you from that" (MSG). Other translations of Proverbs 29:25 inform us that the fear of man proves to be a snare (NIV, NASB, KJV). The Hebrew word translated *snare* means "a snare, trap, bait. The proper understanding of this Hebrew word is the lure or bait placed in a hunter's trap."[6] Our desires to please others ensnare us and inevitably lead us to conform to the peer pressure around us. We must be strong enough to withstand the prodding of the crowds and the pressures of friends. Can we accept being the only ones on God's side even when it means we will lose our Christian friends? Can we withstand others having a wrong impression of us? Can we perform God's will even if it means our reputations before others will be blemished?

Francis Frangipane said, "To inoculate me from the praise of man, he baptized me in the criticism of man, until I died to control of man." This statement is thought-provoking, isn't it? As we seek to please others, it places us under their control. And if we are under their control, then we cannot remain under the LORD's control. We can only have one master. If we seek to please men, we are no longer servants of Christ. In fact, we become the slaves of men. "You were bought at a price; do not become slaves of men" (1 Corinthians 7:23). We have been bought by a price, the precious blood of our LORD; let us not become the slaves of man; let us not become slaves to what others think of us. It is refreshing and exciting not to worry about what others think. It can be very demanding to be subject to another person's expectations, demands, and opinions. We need to remain unaffected by man's praise and undaunted by man's criticism.

Read John 12:42-43 and fill in the blank.
   The Pharisees loved _____ more than _____.

What are some practical measures we can take to stop being people pleasers?

_____

What is our goal (2 Corinthians 5:9)?

_____

Read Jeremiah 31:3. How can focusing on God's amazing love for you keep you from seeking other people's acceptance?

_____

The main goal in our lives is simple—to love the LORD wholeheartedly and to glorify him. We are given freedom in Christ to please him. Whatever we do, we do for his glory and not for the glory of man. So let's make it our goal to please him.

What can we do to stop being people pleasers? First, we need to stop seeking reputations before men. Though we may never admit it to others, some of us seek to defend ourselves and our reputation before people. As soon as we perceive that someone has misjudged us, we step in to correct the other person's impression of us. Augustine prayed, "O LORD, deliver me from this lust of always vindicating myself." We need to lay down our reputations at the foot of the cross and allow the LORD to defend us. When necessary, he will insure we are esteemed before others and will correct their opinions of us. Though it may seem difficult, especially if you are thin skinned like me, let's work on not worrying about what others think of us. "Do not pay attention to every word people say, or you may hear your servant cursing you- for you know in your heart that many times you yourself have cursed others" (Ecclesiastes 7:21-22). Constantly striving to maintain our reputations before others can cripple our Christian walk. Our motivation subtly shifts from pleasing the LORD to pleasing others. If we cling to our reputations before others, in the end, we may lose our reputations before the LORD.

Second, we need to meditate on how much God truly loves us. As we begin to better grasp God's great love for us, we will care less what others think of us; hence, we will stop trying to please others in order to receive their acceptance and affirmation. We have an audience of one, a King of kings and LORD of LORDS. Why do we bow before men, seeking their approval and acceptance? We have a LORD who loves and accepts us unconditionally. Let's rest in his acceptance, relax in his love, and find true peace in his arms. Then the taunts and criticisms of the world are drowned out by the sweetness of his embrace.

Week 5:
Downcast by Disappointment

Day 1: Bruised and Shackled

Day 2: Challenged to Trust

Day 3: Beautiful in Time

Day 4: Lavished with Love

Day 5: The Greatness of God

Key Thoughts for the Week

Day 1: Though others may forget us or forsake us, our LORD always remembers us for he has engraved us on the palms of his hands.

Day 2: We must trust the LORD even when the light turns to darkness and when the mountain top becomes a valley bottom.

Day 3: As we stand at the gates of eternity, everything will seem right.

Day 4: God lavishes his love on us, always seeking our best from an eternal perspective.

Day 5: Reflecting on the greatness of God enables us to move past the hurts and disappointments of this life.

Day 1: Bruised and Shackled

> They bruised his feet with shackles, his neck was put in irons.
>
> Psalm 105:18

In our Christian walk, we will inevitably face disappointments. Circumstances will not go our way. People will let us down. Unforeseen events will occur. We will *all* face disappointments, but how we handle them greatly impacts our joy. We will spend the next few days discussing how to deal with our disappointments in a godly manner. Our lesson will mainly focus on the life of Joseph, the disappointments he faced, and how he dealt with them.

What do the following Scriptures reveal about Joseph?

Genesis 30:22-24 _____

Genesis 37:3 _____

Read Genesis 37 and Genesis 39 and list some possible disappointments that Joseph faced. _____

What are some of the disappointments that you have faced in your life?

_____

Jacob was the grandson of the great patriarch Abraham. He had twelve sons and one daughter; one of these sons was a boy named Joseph. As Genesis 37 opens, Joseph is seventeen years old and full of life. Joseph's brothers, however, are jealous of him. And as a result of their jealousy, they seek to kill Joseph but end up selling him into slavery instead. As we read Joseph's story, our tendency is to casually glance over the fact that Joseph is sold into slavery and move on to the next chapter of his life in Egypt. In doing so, we miss a vital part of Joseph's experiences and the disappointments he suffers. So let's spend a few moments to imagine what it would feel like to be sold into slavery.

- Your own family members sell you into slavery. Not some evil, violent criminals, but your own family, those you love and trust the most. Imagine the isolation, betrayal, and loneliness.

- You have the misfortune of being thrown into a cold, dark well and can hear your brothers deliberating on your fate. Will they cold-bloodedly murder you?

- After your brothers sell you to Midianite merchants, the Midianites place your hands and feet in shackles, and you walk for miles to Egypt. You are now a common slave. Do you retain a seed of hope that perhaps your brothers will acknowledge their wrongdoing and send a search party for you?

- Once in Egypt, the Midianite merchants place you on the slave block and auction you off, like an animal, stripped of dignity and self-respect. As your turn approaches, you wonder where you will end up. What type of owner will purchase you?

- You have now been exposed to a completely different culture in a foreign land, a land you may know little about. You are forced to learn a new language and are indoctrinated into a new way of life. You have been completely removed from the known comforts of home.

- Your new culture overflows with idolatry. Imagine the culture shock of having been reared in a monotheistic culture in which you have only ever worshipped one God and now being exposed to a culture that worships multiple gods.

- You are now a slave in someone else's household. You may be whipped or beaten for your service. Your freedom has been stripped from you. This has become your new life, and you are still at the tender age of seventeen. It is hard to truly grasp the magnitude of the disappointments that Joseph faced, isn't it?

While in Egypt, Joseph faithfully serves his new master, Potiphar, a high-ranking official. The LORD stays with Joseph during this difficult time, and consequently, Joseph prospers in everything he does. Potiphar eventually entrusts care of his entire household to him, what a compliment to Joseph's faithfulness. Things seem to have finally settled down for poor Joseph, but then Potiphar's wife develops an attraction for him and starts trying to seduce him. Genesis 39:6b describes Joseph as well-built and handsome. The Old Testament gives this distinction to only a handful of men: Saul, David, Absalom, and Joseph. Though Joseph is attractive, he is also righteous and refuses to be seduced by Potiphar's wife. Even though she continues after him day after day, he remains righteous in his actions.

Angry at his denial, Potiphar's wife lies about Joseph and causes his imprisonment. This is probably not the reward for righteous behavior that Joseph expects. Yet another heartbreak. Yet another disappointment. After years of faithfully serving his master, Joseph is imprisoned, and not one of the other slaves stands up for him. Surely the rest of the household knows of Potiphar's wife's immoral behavior? What about us—would we bear the reproach for another in telling the truth even if means the dismissal from our job, the loss of a friendship, or our imprisonment?

Joseph's response to the injustice and disappointment is quite amazing, isn't it? Rather than wallowing in the injustice of the situation, he is determined to show those around him the glory of the God he so faithfully worships. And, remember, Joseph is in his late teens, early twenties at the time; he is not a "seasoned" veteran who has walked with the LORD for years. This makes his faithfulness even more amazing.

Read Genesis 39:20-23. Does God remain with Joseph in prison?

☐ Yes   ☐ No

What insight about Joseph's prison life do you find in Psalm 105:17-18?

_____

Fill in the blanks - Hebrews 13:5.

God has said, "_____ will I _____ you; _____ will I _____ you.

Read Genesis 40 and list other disappointments that Joseph faced.

_____

Challenge

What encouragement do you receive from Isaiah 41:10 and Isaiah 49:15-16?

_____

Joseph's imprisonment is neither easy, nor comfortable. The LORD, however, remains with Joseph. No matter what we face, our LORD always remains with us. He is our *Jehovah Shammah*, the LORD is there (Ezekiel 48:35). No matter how isolated and alone we may feel at times, we can always experience the LORD's comforting presence. "God has said, 'Never will I leave you; never will I forsake you' " (Hebrews 13:5).

While in prison, the LORD shows kindness to Joseph and grants him favor in the eyes of the warden. As a result, the warden places Joseph in charge of the prisoners. Does this sound familiar? The same thing happened while Joseph served Potiphar. Genesis 40 also informs us that Joseph prospers while in prison, refusing to become a victim of his circumstances. He makes the best of his situation, and in this instance, becomes the "best" prisoner. Let's reflect on that for a moment. Joseph prospers, not as a CEO of a company, living in luxury, and experiencing a comfortable life, but rather as a prison inmate, having his most basic needs met. What a wonderful reminder to us that the LORD can enable us to experience joy no matter our circumstances. Remember our circumstances do not dictate our level of joy; our relationship with our LORD does.

While in prison, Joseph meets two interesting men, a baker and a cupbearer. A cupbearer was a man who tasted the king's drink to make sure it was not poisonous. Both of these men have unusual dreams, and Joseph helps to interpret their dreams. He explains that within three days, the baker will die while the cupbearer will be restored to his original position. Joseph asks the cupbearer to remember him. Since the cupbearer tastes the king's drink, he has access to the king and can seek Joseph's release. After eleven years of being a slave and a prisoner, a glimmer of hope has finally appeared.

But just as suddenly as the glimmer of hope appears, so suddenly it dies, for the cupbearer forgets Joseph. Yet another disappointment. Yet another heartache. Though the cupbearer forgets poor Joseph, God has not, and God is working out his deliverance, though Joseph does not know it. Though family may forget us and friends may forsake us, our LORD always remembers us, *always*. He has engraved us on the palms of his hands (Isaiah 49:15-16).

Though the circumstances *seem* to be against Joseph, he never loses hope for he knows that his LORD is working things out for his deliverance. He knows that God will never leave him, nor forsake him. No matter the situation we face, no matter how hopeless it seems, we too must never lose hope. Our magnificent LORD is working things out for our good and for his glory. He walks with us daily to give us the strength and grace we need, even through the hardest of times.

Day 2: Challenged to Trust

> Trust in the LORD with all your heart and lean not on your own understanding.
>
> Proverbs 3:5

During times of disappointment, it is so important that we continue to trust our LORD. And yet trust during these times is so difficult, isn't it? Everything in us screams against trusting the LORD, but we must often do the exact opposite of our emotions if we wish to experience enduring joy.

How do you *normally* handle the disappointments in your life?

_____

How does Joseph respond to the disappointments in his life (Genesis 50:20)?

_____

What do the following verses reveal about trusting the LORD?
Psalm 9:9-10 _____
Psalm 62:5-8 _____

During times of disappointment, does your trust in the LORD remain steadfast or does it waver?
☐ Wavers   ☐ Steadfast   ☐ Explain _____

Challenge
Read Exodus 13:17-18. When God delivers the Israelites from Egypt, why does he take the Israelites on the longer path? Apply this to why you may sometimes face disappointments.

_____

Disappointment is a normal part of our Christian walk and can take many forms. Sometimes it comes as not receiving the promotion we expected, having a friend divulge our personal information, or having a spouse cheat on us. At other times it comes through the unexpected loss of a loved one, a wayward child, or the gossip of a neighbor. Though disappointments may naturally arise, they create a great crossroad for us. We can either pour out our hearts to the LORD and continue to trust him, or we can dwell on the disappointment and become embittered by it. If we choose the latter, we can easily enter a season of discouragement or despair and can unknowingly allow the chains of self-pity to bind us.

So how do we keep from being discouraged? We pray to our LORD. He can provide us with the wisdom that we need to handle the disappointment and discernment for what to do next. Our prayer should be honest—we should openly share our feelings with the LORD. The LORD knows how crushing some of our disappointments are. Let's allow the God of all comfort to comfort us during these times. "The LORD is close to the brokenhearted and saves those who are crushed in spirit" (Psalm 34:18).

Even if we cannot understand why a result happened the way it did, we should still be honest with the LORD and allow him to give us wisdom. For example, a friend of ours worked as an attorney and lost his job. During this same time, he and his wife had a new baby girl. His wife was on maternity leave with her company and hoping to stay home with their new baby, but their need for medical insurance necessitated her returning to work. Ten days before she had to return to work, her husband received a job interview with a prestigious law firm, a seemingly perfect job. He went through four rounds of interviews only to finally discover that he did not receive the job. Everything had seemed to line up so perfectly. Have you ever been there, where you perceived God's will as one thing, and then it turned out to be something completely different? Wouldn't it have been easier for the LORD to let my friend get rejected in the first interview instead of allowing his hopes to rise through the three successive interviews? Why even interview at all; why not bring the perfect job right away? These are the questions that plague us. We cannot understand God at times and why he chooses certain paths for us. He certainly seems to take us around the long path a lot, doesn't he? Remember the Israelites when God delivered them from Egypt. Rather than taking them the shorter and more direct path, he made them take the longer and windier path. Why? Because they were not militarily strong enough to defeat the enemies that they would encounter in the shorter path. The LORD always knows the best path for us, though it may seem contrary to what we think. There are obstacles in our shorter paths that we could never conquer because we are not spiritually mature enough. He leads us down the longer path, though it may be more tedious and tiring, in order to protect us. And yet we experience disappointment, don't we, because we often expect to follow the shorter and seemingly easier path but then end up with the longer and more trying path. It is during these times of disappointment, when things seem so uncertain and so difficult, that we must trust God the most. "Those who know your name will trust in you, for you, LORD, have never forsaken those who seek you" (Psalm 9:10).

Personalize my paraphrase of Proverbs 3:5-6 by filling in the blanks.
I, _____, will trust in the LORD with _____ my heart when I face a disappointment. I will not _____ on my own understanding because it is limited and one dimensional. I will not turn to my own resources because they are finite and small. In all my ways, I will _____ you because I know that you will make my _____. I know that you have a plan for me that far surpasses even my greatest imagination so I will trust in you no matter what.

It is easy to trust God when things are going well in our lives—when we have the houses we desire, possess the perfect jobs, or are married to great spouses—but what happens when our children develop cancer or our spouses are laid off? Do we still trust God when the disappointments of life seem overwhelming? Proverbs 3:5-6 reminds us to trust in the LORD and to not lean on our own understanding. The Hebrew word for *trust* means "to lie helpless, facedown. It pictures a servant waiting for the master's command in readiness to obey or a defeated soldier yielding himself to the conquering general."[1] God desires for us to express this same trust in him and in his ability to resolve our situation. The LORD is completely trustworthy. He has never failed us nor let us down, and he never will. We must learn to trust him even when the light turns to darkness and when the mountain top becomes a valley bottom.

Exercise

During times of disappointment, Satan secretly whispers some of his greatest lies, and we are prone to believe him because of our vulnerable state. Let's arm ourselves with the great truths of God in order to combat Satan's lies. Read through the list on the following page and look up any areas which apply to you.

God does not love you or he would not have allowed you to experience this disappointment.	1 John 3:1
God will eventually leave you.	Matthew 28:20b
God has forgotten about you or he would have answered your prayer by now.	Isaiah 49:14-16
God will not forgive you, not this time.	1 John 1:9
You are asking for the impossible.	Luke 18:27
Your fears are reasonable.	2 Timothy 1:7

Which of Satan's lies do you tend to succumb to the most? Why?

It is during times of disappointment that Satan seems to wreak havoc with many of us. And because we are in such a fragile and vulnerable state, we are most susceptible to him. So he secretly whispers some of his greatest lies to us. Fear, doubt, confusion, unbelief, guilt, shame—these are some of the fiery darts that Satan throws at us. We must use our shields of faith to deflect Satan's darts, or we will succumb to his vicious schemes.

Perhaps one of Satan's greatest techniques is to create doubt in our minds. Has God abandoned me? Why has God allowed this to happen? How can God allow me to experience this disappointment and still love me? Slowly Satan's whispers become seductive enticements. We should have stopped listening at the first whisper, but we didn't. Now we're down the well-worn path of doubt, doubt about God's love for us and doubt about our Christian walk. Slowly our doubt leads to unbelief, and unbelief is no small sin. It kept the Israelites in the dessert for forty years and kept Zechariah silent during the entirety of Elizabeth's pregnancy (Luke 1:5-25). We must realize that Satan has devious schemes, and we must remain on guard. Our great defense during times like this is the truth of God's Word and the power of God's promises.

Day 3: Beautiful in Time

> He has made everything beautiful in its time.
>
> Ecclesiastes 3:11a

These past few days have shown us that Joseph's life has not been easy. He has suffered one disappointment after another. Life has certainly not turned out the way he envisioned. What child thinks that he will be sold into slavery by his own brothers and then imprisoned in a foreign country? But Joseph's day of redemption has finally arrived.

Read Genesis 41 and answer the following questions.

What series of events does the LORD use to deliver Joseph?

_____

For how long does Joseph serve as a slave and prisoner before his release by Pharaoh (hint: compare Genesis 37:2 with Genesis 41:46)? _____

Describe Joseph as he stands before Pharaoh. _____

Have you ever experienced a disappointment that was the result of wrong timing? Explain.

_____

Sometimes we experience disappointment because the timing is not right. Joseph, for example, remains in prison for an additional two years after the cupbearer promises to remember him—two full years, as Scripture so nicely describes, seven hundred thirty excruciatingly long days after he thinks he might be delivered. But during that time God is placing the finishing touches on Joseph. He is perfecting Joseph's character and preparing him for his new place of service. Sometimes we are not ready for God's plans for us (though, of course, we think we are). J. Oswald Sanders has insightfully remarked, "Not every man can carry a full cup. Sudden elevation frequently leads to pride and a fall."[2] Joseph will remain a slave and a prisoner for thirteen long, hard years before the Lord will elevate him. But in those years, Joseph will grow in humility, selflessness, and love for his Lord.

Joseph's character becomes evident as he stands before Pharaoh. Pharaoh has experienced two dreams, and none of his magicians can interpret them. The magicians were intellectual and learned men, yet they cannot provide Pharaoh an answer. So Pharaoh summons Joseph. Joseph has waited patiently and now finally tastes freedom. And once things begin to happen, they happen at a whirlwind pace. Isn't that just how it happens with God? We wait and wait, and then all of a sudden, things seem to occur in overdrive.

So there stands Joseph before one of the greatest men of his time. Do you notice the beauty of his response to Pharaoh? "'I cannot do it,' Joseph replies to Pharaoh, 'but God will give Pharaoh the answer he desires'" (Genesis 41:16). Joseph's moment has arrived; he now stands before one of the most powerful men in the world. What a temptation to glorify himself instead of the Lord. But the years have humbled Joseph tremendously, and he points Pharaoh to the Lord. Joseph demonstrates his humility again when he instructs Pharaoh to place a wise and discerning man in charge of everything but does not advocate himself.[3] Wouldn't we at least suggest ourselves for the position, even if nonchalantly? But not Joseph. He informs Pharaoh what to do and then stands back and trusts God.

What a contrast to the world in which we live; people push, they manipulate, they jockey for position, trying to place themselves forward. How much sweeter it would be if they allowed the LORD to elevate them instead of trying to artificially elevate themselves. "For everyone who exalts himself will be humbled, and he who humbles himself will be exalted" (Luke 18:14).

Joseph probably does not even realize it, but God has been cultivating him all along for this position in both his character, which we just discussed, and in his abilities. Remember, when Joseph was sold to Potiphar, he managed all of Potiphar's household affairs. Then in prison, again Joseph managed the affairs for the prison— more responsibility and a further development of his abilities.[4] Now God will use those management abilities to enable Joseph to rule Egypt as second in command. Imagine at thirty years old having the privilege of being second in command of a nation. Imagine all that the position would bring—wealth, influence, power, luxury, prestige, women. All of these could easily have corrupted Joseph if he were not securely grounded in his LORD, but thirteen years as a slave and prisoner has served as his school, and he has learned well. At thirty years old, Joseph enjoys all the privileges of his new position yet never strays from his love and devotion to the LORD.

I also love how God delivers Joseph by using Pharaoh's dreams. Thirteen years earlier, Joseph's dream-telling ability caused him to be sold into slavery, but now the LORD uses that same ability to deliver him. And do you notice how perfect the timing is? Two years earlier, Joseph had probably experienced disappointment that the cupbearer forgot him, but the timing was not right. If the cupbearer had remembered Joseph and brought him before Pharaoh, it would probably have been more out of idle curiosity than a need; and after satisfying Pharaoh's curiosity, Joseph may have been sent back to prison.[5] Joseph certainly would not have had the opportunity to display the true *Jehovah God* and contrast the wise men of Egypt.[6] God designed it as only he could, perfectly. Though we may be initially disappointed with an outcome, we must realize that

God has a greater plan for us, and he knows the right timing. As we stand at the gates of eternity, everything will seem right. "He has made everything beautiful in its time" (Ecclesiastes 3:11a).

Do disappointments discourage you? Why or why not?

_____

According to Romans 5:3-5, hope never

_____

What encouragement do you receive from Lamentations 3:24-25?

_____

How can maintaining an eternal perspective help us to deal with our disappointments?

_____

Sometimes we become disappointed and discouraged for the wrong reasons, such as the ones listed below:

- *We possess unrealistic expectations.* Sometimes we expect God to provide what we want when that is not consistent with his eternal plan. It is very easy to become disillusioned with God when things do not turn out the way we expect. And the greater the gap in expectation, the greater the disappointment. Yet, we stand at such a limited, earthly vantage point. Only the LORD possesses the full, eternal picture. Sometimes his ways will seem contrary to us. Disappointments provide us a great opportunity to re-evaluate our plans and determine if perhaps we have focused on the wrong things, earthly things instead of eternal things.

- *We use the wrong standard.* Sometimes we misjudge an outcome based on an earthly standard. For example, assume I diligently plan an in-home Bible study for months. If only two couples attend, I may become unnecessarily discouraged, feeling that God has not answered my prayers. In reality, the LORD may have sent me only two couples so that I could have a deeper fellowship with them and discuss more intimate areas. In this instance, I have unintentionally used the wrong measuring stick, creating unnecessary disappointment and frustration in my life. We should not become discouraged because we do not receive the results we desire but must always leave the results to the LORD. What we judge as failure, and consequently what can create great discouragement in us, God may judge as success.

- *We forget God's great power.* Sometimes we allow circumstances to overwhelm us and forget that our great Redeemer and Provider stands ready to help us. There is no obstacle so great and no difficulty so large that God cannot overcome it. Hear the encouraging words that God spoke to the Israelites: "I will make rivers flow on barren heights, and springs within the valleys. I will turn the desert into pools of water, and the parched ground into springs" (Isaiah 41:17-18). God will make a way, where there is no way. Some of us are in barren lands, but God will bring us the springs of life that we need. The LORD has innovative ways to answer our problems, so we should not become discouraged when things do not seem to happen as we plan.

- *We place hope in the wrong object, for instance in a person or a job.* Scripture never really shows Joseph complaining or discouraged. Though Joseph has experienced great disappointments, he never seems to experience great discouragement. Why? Because his hope is never in his circumstances, in other people, or in fate. His hope remains fixed in the LORD, and hope in the LORD never disappoints. Joseph understands God's sovereign guiding hand in his life and hopes in him. He understands that God can work for the good of those who love him through acts of evil. "You intended to harm me, but God intended it for good to accomplish what is now being done, the saving of many lives" (Genesis 50:20). What our enemies use to hurt us, God can use to help us, if we allow him to. He is sovereignly working out all things for our good and for his glory.

Whether we realize it or not, disappointments have the potential to help us grow and mature in our Christian walk. God will use our disappointments to build character in our lives and to mold us into the godly people we were meant to be, but we must trust the LORD and his wonderful plans for us.

Day 4: Lavished with Love

> How great is the love the Father has lavished on us, that we should be called children of God!
>
> 1 John 3:1a

One of the reasons that our disappointments frequently turn to discouragement and sometimes even despair is because we do not understand how much the LORD truly loves us and how much he seeks our best. Let's spend today better understanding God's love for us.

According to 1 John 3:1, what has God lavished on us?
☐ His mercy   ☐ His holiness   ☐ His love

Read Zephaniah 3:17. Do you picture God lavishing his love on you and rejoicing over you in singing? Place an X on the box below that applies to you.
☐ Have never imagined it   ☐ Only occasionally picture it
☐ Bask in God's love

What do the following verses reveal about God's love for us?

Isaiah 54:10 _____

Matthew 10:29-31 _____

What interesting insight do you find in Psalm 56:8 (use NASB if possible)?

_____

How did God demonstrate his love for us (1 John 4:10)?

_____

During times of disappointment, we need to cling to God's great love for us. "How great is the love the Father has lavished on us, that we should be called children of God" (1 John 3:1a). God loves us passionately and unconditionally. He demonstrated this amazing love for us on the cross (John 3:16, 1 John 4:10). No matter how much Satan whispers in our dark moments that God does not love us, he does, and the cross is our great reminder. Nothing will alter God's love for us, and nothing will separate us from his love, nothing—not hardship, not persecution, not famine, not danger, not even death (Romans 8:35-39).

God's love for us is infinite, meaning it knows no bounds. Even in sin, which is utter defiance against God, he still loves us, and he loves us the same as when we are good, obedient children. His love is absolutely unconditional. Though God knows all of our faults and failings, and though he sees our sin, he loves us anyway. Let us revel in the fact that God loves us regardless of how sinful we are and how many times we fail him; let us stop trying to hide who we truly are and allow the Holy Spirit to conform us to the people God desires us to be.

Sometimes we perceive the LORD as an angry tyrant, just waiting for us to sin so that he can chastise us. Or perhaps he is some distant cosmic force, disengaged from our lives. Yet the LORD takes an active interest in our lives, always seeking our best. Psalm 56:8 (NASB) reminds us, "You have taken account of my wanderings; Put my tears in your bottle Are they not in your book?" What a beautiful visual for us. God is not indifferent to our sadness and pain. He takes note of every hurt that we have suffered and every tear that we have shed.

What encouragement do you receive from Romans 8:31-32?

_____

As you experience disappointments in life, do you sometimes think God is against you (be honest)? Circle the answer that best describes you.

Frequently   Sometimes   Rarely

Read Psalm 84:11. Will God withhold something that is in our best interest? How does this encourage you?

_____

Some of us "know" that God loves us, and yet we have never really received that love. Though we have heard it and may have even memorized Scriptures about it, we have never really allowed it to dwell in our hearts and to penetrate our souls. For whatever reason, and we each have our own different reasons, we simply do not believe that God loves us, especially during those times of darkness. But God's love for us is not just some Biblical doctrine, it is one of life's most beautiful and comforting realities. We must become secure in God's love for us, or we will succumb to the deceitful whispers of Satan. "And I pray that you, being rooted and established in love, may have power, together with all the saints, to grasp how wide and long and high and deep is the love of Christ, and to know this love that surpasses knowledge—that you may be filled to the measure of all the fullness of God" (Ephesians 3:17b-19). Oh that we would grasp how wide, how long, how high, and how truly deep the love Christ has for us.

Romans 8:31 tells us that God is *for us*. Let me say it again so that it truly penetrates our hearts because during those difficult times of disappointment, when the heartbreak is great and the pain is overwhelming, we forget that God is for us, don't we? And yet, God is for us, during the brightest moments of our lives and during the darkest ones. God is for us no matter the circumstances that surround us, seeking our best and moving us from glory to greater glory. God does not stand in heaven pitted against us, intentionally creating pain and hurt in our lives. He is lovingly walking with us and enabling us to stand strong. Whatever he allows in our lives, he allows for our good and for his glory. Romans 8:32 reminds us that God gave us his best–he gave us his son. There is nothing more that God can do to demonstrate that he loves us. If, as sinners and enemies, God gave us his best, then now as his beloved children, how would he not give us all that we need? The answer then is simple—if God does not provide it, it is not because God does not love us, but rather that it is not in our *eternal* best interest. Though we are often willing to settle, God is not. He loves us far too much to give us anything less than the best.

No one loves us as much as God does or seeks our well being as much as God. Zephaniah 3:17 reminds us that the Lord rejoices over us with singing. The Hebrew word *suws*, translated *rejoice*, means "to rejoice; to exalt; to be glad. It is a verb that indicates great rejoicing and jubilant celebration."[7] This is how much the Lord loved the Israelites and how much he loves us. Can you picture the Lord in jubilant celebration over you? Can you picture him lavishing his love on you? As you experience your next disappointment, remember God's great love for you. It will make the disappointment so much more bearable.

What is God's love letter to the Israelites in Jeremiah 29:11?

_____

If we let him, what can God do with our heartbreaks and disappointments?

Psalm 30:11-12 _____

Isaiah 66:13 _____

Has God ever taken one of your past disappointments and brought victory out of it? Explain.

_____

Ecclesiastes 7:8 reminds us, "the end of a matter is better than its beginning." Joseph, for example, started as a slave but ended up as an official in Pharaoh's court. We cannot always trust the visible circumstances around us. God is working for a much greater purpose than we can see or imagine. Our earthly vision can only take us so far. In his commentary on Ecclesiastes, Warren Wiersbe interestingly notes that Satan starts with the "best" but then leads us down a path of pain and misery, while God often saves the "best" for last.[8] Those words ring so true, don't they? Satan uses deceit and subterfuge to mask his temptations to appear wonderful in the beginning; but we soon face the painful consequences. The LORD, on the other hand, often uses what seems a difficult and heartbreaking situation and then brings beauty and good out of it.

God has such great plans for each of us. In Jeremiah 29:11, God sends a love letter to the Israelites, telling them that he plans to prosper them and give them hope for a future. The Israelites will endure a brutal enslavement and seventy long, hard years of exile, but after that time, God promises that he will restore them to their land and give them a wonderful future. No matter the disappointments that we face, the LORD has a wonderful plan for our future as well. He always seeks our good *from an eternal perspective*. And he will never waste one hurt that we have experienced. For example, my husband and I have friends that were unable to have children. Though this was initially a crushing blow, they chose to rest in God. Eventually they adopted two babies who needed love and security. God took one of their greatest disappointments and used it to bring victory in their lives and in the lives of two innocent children. As God allows disappointments in our lives, it is not so that these disappointments will dishearten us, but rather that we receive his greater blessing. In our own wisdom and will, we would naively select a lesser blessing. We must trust God for the perfect ending. It will come, whether in this lifetime or the next. Out of some of our deepest and most sorrowful disappointments will come some of our greatest and most wondrous triumphs.

Day 5: The Greatness of God

> How great you are, O Sovereign LORD! There is no one like you, and there is no God but you, as we have heard with our own ears.
>
> 2 Samuel 7:22

Keeping our joy during times of disappointment is always challenging. This week, we have studied how to retain our joy in spite of our circumstances: 1) continue to trust in the LORD, 2) remember that God makes everything beautiful in his time, and 3) reflect on the LORD's great love for us. Today, we will discuss the final element – focusing on the greatness of God and his glory.

Read 2 Samuel 7:1-17 about a disappointment in David's life and answer the following questions.

What does David want to do?_____

What is God's response? _____

Do you think David's desire arose from a pure heart (1 Kings 8:18)?
☐ Yes　　　　　☐ No

Can you recall an instance when you desired something but God answered No?

_____

Though God says No, how does he encourage David (2 Samuel 7:8-16)?

_____

As David settles in his palace and experiences rest from his ene-mies, he sets his heart on building the LORD his temple, a perma-nent place of worship. David has already restored the Ark of the Covenant to its rightful place in Jerusalem and now seeks the noble goal of building a permanent home for it (2 Samuel 6). The LORD, however, has other plans. Though the LORD commends David's heart and motive, he does not allow him to build the temple; this distinction will be given to his son Solomon. Imagine King David's great disappointment. He has set his heart on a noble aspiration, and yet the LORD says no. Sometimes, we face similar disappoint-ments. Perhaps we are trying to find the right spouses or have been praying for years to have children. Yet the LORD's answer is no. No matter how noble our goal or how right our desire seems, some-times it is not in our LORD's plan for us. With our earthly wisdom and emotions, we cannot quite fathom the LORD's plan, and yet we must trust him.

Though the LORD denies David his goal, he encourages him by reminding him that he will make his name great and will establish the throne of his kingdom forever, known as the Davidic Covenant. Rather than allowing David to build him a house, God will instead build David's house. Even when the LORD says no to us, he tenderly and lovingly provides encouragement if we will pay attention. We must also remember that just because the LORD says no to us does not mean that he does not love us. God's denial does not mean that he does not love David or that he loves Solomon more but rather that it does not fit in with God's eternal plans. Can you think of an instance when the LORD provided you needed encouragement after a great disappointment?

Continue reading 2 Samuel 7:18-24 and answer the following questions.

How does David respond to God's No? _____

How does David address God? _____

How does David describe himself? _____

On whom does David focus?   □ God   □ Himself

During times of disappointment, on whom do you normally focus?
□ Focus more on self   □ Focus more on God

What do you learn about the greatness of God from the following verses?

Exodus 15:11 _____

Isaiah 40:25-26 _____

How can focusing on the LORD keep you from becoming discouraged and disillusioned?

_____

David's immediate response to God's no is quite remarkable, isn't it? He humbly bows before the LORD's will and accepts his lot. He does not argue with God or try to plead his case. He simply accepts God's no, even though it is his heart's great desire.

In his response to God, David focuses on the greatness of God. First, he acknowledges the LORD's great sovereignty. He addresses the LORD as *Jehovah Adonai*, which means Sovereign LORD, and *Jehovah Elohim*, which emphasizes God's power. David knows the LORD has plans that far surpass his earthly wisdom and understanding.

David also emphasizes his own unworthiness. Who is David that the LORD will allow him to have a kingdom? He is nothing more than a shepherd, but God's great mercy has enabled him to be a king. And who are we that the LORD gives us what he gives us. We were all sinners destined for hell until our loving LORD chose to redeem us and give us new lives. "When I consider your heavens, the work of your fingers, the moon and the stars, which you have set in place, what is man that you are mindful of him, the son of man that you care for him?" (Psalm 8:3-4). As we face disappointments in life, we must remain focused on our LORD and his magnificence. "How great you are, O Sovereign LORD! There is no one like you, and there is no God but you" (2 Samuel 7:22).

Disappointments have the tendency to remove our focus from the LORD and place it on ourselves. And yet, the more we focus on ourselves and our situation, the more discouraged we will become. Reflecting on the greatness of God enables us to move past the hurts and disappointments of this life. Unfortunately, the busyness of life often keeps us from reflecting on God, and we may unintentionally downplay him and his magnificence, sometimes even humanizing him to our terms. Yet if we would spend more time reflecting on who he truly is, it would create immense awe and reverence in us. For example, consider some of the following attributes of God and how they demonstrate his greatness:

Infinity - God is infinite, which means he is unlimited and knows no bounds (Job 11:7–9, 1 Kings 8:27). God is unlimited by time, unrestricted by space, and boundless in the depth of his attributes. We will spend all of eternity learning about God and yet still never fully know him because he is infinite. Yet God fully knows himself. Take a moment and truly absorb that. God has no bounds because he is infinite, yet he fully knows himself. Our minds reel as we struggle to grasp how a being who has no bounds can still be fully known.

Eternity – God has no beginning, nor end. He is from all eternity (Psalm 93:2, Psalm 10:12, 1 Chronicles 16:36). God has always existed. There has never been a time God has not existed. In fact, "time" as we understand it cannot be applied to God since God created time. Time, like space and matter, is a creation of God. Time is not a succession of events for God for he sees all events with equal vividness. Thus, he can view the past, present, and future simultaneously. So for instance, before I existed, God existed. Before creation existed, God existed. Before time existed, God existed. Imagine, as created beings, we rely on time; we cannot exist apart from the dimension of time as it pertains to events in our lives, and yet God exists outside of time.

Immutability – God does not change in essence or being (Psalm 102:25-27, Malachi 3:6, Hebrews 13:8). God does not change with respect to his essence because there is no reason for him to change. He is already perfect, and he is perfect in every area. There is no area in life in which God needs to advance himself. He does not need to grow and mature over time. He does not need to gain wisdom or acquire knowledge because he has always possessed all wisdom necessary for all eternity. Imagine God has never changed, not in one instance, not for one moment. We can do nothing but change, and yet God has never changed.

This is but a wisp of God. He is truly magnificent. "I am God, and there is no other; I am God, and there is none like me" (Isaiah 46:9). In a moment, the whirlwind of life can destroy all that we hold dear, the most precious things we possess. In that moment, we will need to cling desperately to the Lord. But we cannot cling to someone we do not know. As we come to better know God, we will stand transfixed by his greatness and overwhelmed by his majesty; then our disappointments and heartbreaks will seem far more bearable. This is what enables us to experience joy in this lifetime even though we may experience disappointments with how circumstances have turned out. Too many times the disappointments of this life overwhelm us because we have shifted our eyes from the magnificence of our Lord to the inward gaze of our disappointment. We focus on the earthly instead of the eternal. Let's instead stand in silence and gaze at the beauty and magnificence of our Lord, for he is truly amazing! "Now to the King eternal, immortal, invisible, the only God, be honor and glory for ever and ever. Amen" (1 Timothy 1:17).

Week 6:
Imprisoned by Unforgiveness

Day 1: Forgiving the Unforgivable

Day 2: Channels of Mercy

Day 3: Betrayed by Blood

Day 4: A Bitter Root

Day 5: Perfect Justice

Key Thoughts for the Week

Day 1:   With God living in us, we have the power to forgive others just as Christ forgave us.

Day 2:   The heart of forgiveness rests on our understanding of how much we have been forgiven.

Day 3:   Revenge and retaliation are never the answer—they only create greater problems and more issues.

Day 4:   Once the seed of bitterness takes root, it produces its sour fruit, imprisoning us by turning our gaze inwards and poisoning our lives with self-pity.

Day 5:   In forgiving others, we allow God, as our protector and avenger, to administer perfect justice and to right our wrongs.

Day 1: Forgiving the Unforgivable

> Bear with each other and forgive whatever grievances you may
> have against one another. Forgive as the LORD forgave you.
>
> Colossians 3:13

"Every one says forgiveness is a lovely idea, until they have something to forgive."[1] That is so true, isn't it? We easily embrace forgiveness and mercy when we have offended others, and yet that
same forgiveness and mercy doesn't seem quite as nice when we
are the offended party. Forgiveness often serves as one of the most
challenging areas in our Christian walk, for it tests the convictions
of our hearts. Second Peter 1:4 informs us that we are partakers of
the divine nature, and nothing reveals this nature more than forgiving what seems almost unforgivable.

Read Matthew 18:21-22. What do you learn about forgiveness?

_____

What additional insight do you receive from 1 Corinthians 13:5?
    It [love] is not rude, it is not self-seeking, it is not easily angered,
    it _____.

Do you tend to keep track of people's offenses? Do their old offenses
seem to surface during new conflicts with them? Explain.

_____

In Matthew 18, Jesus provides a poignant parable on the importance
of forgiveness. Peter, in his usual headstrong manner, approaches
Jesus and asks him how many times he has to forgive his brother.
The rabbis of the day only required Jews to forgive an offense three
times. Once a person committed his fourth offense, his duty to forgive his offender ended. Thus, as Peter inquires about forgiveness,

he doubles the required amount of times to forgive to seven times, perhaps thinking that he is being generous.

No doubt Jesus's answer probably surprises Peter. Peter most likely expects Jesus to praise him for his gracious piety, but instead Jesus mildly rebukes him. Jesus answers not seven times, but seventy times seven. In answering Peter, Jesus is not implying that we should maintain a ledger of each person's faults against us, and when we reach 491 to stop forgiving them. Instead, Jesus wants us to practice forgiveness where if we have forgiven someone 490 times, we would be in the habit of extending forgiveness. First Corinthians 13:5 reminds us that love keeps no record of wrongs. The Greek word *logizomai*, translated *account*, means "to count, to occupy oneself with reckonings or calculations."[2] We do not carefully maintain a ledger of the wrongs committed against us or keep score of another's sins. If we truly love our neighbors as ourselves, we do not worry about how many times they have grievously injured us. We forgive their offenses an unlimited number of times. Love extends grace to others when they fall. It helps bear their burdens and forgives what seems unforgivable.

Read Matthew 18:23-35, a parable about forgiveness, and answer the following questions.

Compare the king's treatment of the first servant with the first servant's treatment of the second servant. _____

How do the other servants respond to the first servant's actions?
_____

What eventually happens to the first servant? _____

Do you think forgiveness is easy? Is it costly? Explain.
_____

Have you experienced any of the costs of unforgiveness?
☐ Loss of joy/peace ☐ Anger/bitterness ☐ Worry/anxiety
☐ Discouragement ☐ Sense of hopelessness ☐ Depression

What somber warning do we receive about not forgiving others from Matthew 6:12-15?

_____

To further explain about forgiveness, Jesus shares a parable about two servants and the debts they owe. The first servant owes a debt of ten thousand talents to the king. Since money values fluctuate over time, it is difficult to translate the ten thousand talents to an exact dollar amount. But it certainly represents a sizable amount; some scholars assume a number over ten million dollars in today's money.[3] Jesus's main point is the debt is large and unpayable.

Unable to pay the debt, the servant falls on his knees before the king and pleads for mercy. The king, having compassion and pity on the man, totally cancels the debt and frees him. This act would have stunned Jesus's audience, just as it should stun us. The king does not just offer the servant an extension of time or establish an installment plan. He fully cancels the debt. The king also does not begrudgingly extinguish the debt. He forgives the debt freely and completely.

Can you imagine the exhilaration and joy the servant feels? Never in his wildest imagination could he have envisioned the king forgiving his entire debt. Rather than basking in such elation, however, the first servant finds a second servant who owes him a menial amount, one hundred denarii, and demands repayment, even choking the poor servant. The amount the second servant owes him is insignificant compared to the great amount that he is forgiven, but that does not stop the first servant. The second servant falls to his knees and begs for a little more time to repay the money. Sounds familiar, doesn't it? Surely this plea of mercy will resonate in the first servant's mind since he used similar words before the king. But the first servant's response is quite surprising. He refuses to grant leniency and mercy to this fellow servant and has him imprisoned, a common practice for debtors at that time. Not only does the first servant not forgive the second servant, but he does not even offer the second servant an extension of time to repay the debt or a reduced debt amount. And imprisonment served as the harshest of punishments, for it usually meant the debtor would have no means to repay the debt since he could no longer work. Notice also that the first instance involves a king forgiving a servant, but the second instance only entails a servant forgiving another servant—men on equal footing. The first servant's behavior seems quite shocking. His response seems harsh and callous, devoid of any mercy or grace. How could the first servant who experienced such great forgiveness, the exoneration of such a large debt, then not forgive such a small debt? And how can we, having experienced forgiveness for *all* our sins against a holy God, then not forgive an injustice done to us?

It takes a while to absorb this parable. And perhaps even longer when we realize the application the parable has for us. The king represents God, and the servant symbolizes us. God has demonstrated immense mercy to us and forgiven us the enormous debt of our sin through salvation. And yet we sometimes refuse to forgive others who sin against us. Though we have received great forgiveness, we do not generously offer it to others.

I must clarify that there are different severities of grievances committed against us. Some offenses annoy us; others leave us devastated. Making a rude comment to me is far less significant than stealing my belongings or assaulting me physically. There are various degrees of hurt we endure. The greater the degree of the injury against us, the greater the degree of forgiveness needed; and such forgiveness can only come from our LORD. It is not within our capacity to truly forgive someone who has hurt us deeply. Only the LORD can provide the forgiving spirit and peace. But God's grace is sufficient for all we endure, even the most heinous of crimes (2 Corinthians 12:9). As we speak of forgiveness this week, I am in no way discounting the immense pain and suffering that some of us have experienced. My heart breaks for what some of us have had to endure. Please hear my heart: I am not saying that forgiveness is easy; it is not. But I am saying that the LORD commands us to forgive all the injuries against us and will provide the grace and strength we need to do so. Only through the LORD can we move beyond the immediate hurt and pain of the offense.

Forgiveness is not easy. It is often hard and costly. It was costly for Jesus to forgive our sins, and it will be costly for us to forgive other people's offenses against us. But if we believe that forgiveness is costly, then unforgiveness is even costlier because unforgiveness always imprisons us. Imagine an offense has been committed against you. If you choose not to forgive, you are willingly walking into a jail cell and remaining imprisoned. All the while, your offender may be freely living his life. Unforgiveness holds *us* hostage, not our offender. Some of us need to unlock our prison doors by using the key of forgiveness.

The unmercifulness of the first servant deeply grieves and saddens the other servants so they report his behavior to the king. The king is *moved to anger*. Does that surprise you? The king then summons the first servant, calls him wicked, and turns him over to the jailers for torture. It is also interesting that the king calls the servant wicked. We tend to associate wickedness with sins such as murder, rape, or theft, but unforgiveness? Surely God sees the hurts committed against us and overlooks our unforgiving hearts? No, we cannot readily accept forgiveness from our heavenly Father only to remain unmerciful and unforgiving to those around us.

Our natural flesh rebels against forgiveness, doesn't it? We feel our rights have been violated, and we have the right to even the score. And yet one of the great hallmarks of Christians is their forgiving dispositions. C. S. Lewis said, "To be a Christian means to forgive the inexcusable, because God has forgiven the inexcusable in you."[4] With God living in us, we have the power to forgive others just as Christ has forgiven us.

Day 2: Channels of Mercy

> He has showed you, O man, what is good. And what does the LORD require of you? To act justly and to love mercy and to walk humbly with your God.
>
> Micah 6:8

Yesterday we started studying a parable on forgiveness, but because of its richness and depth, we were not able to complete it. Today, we will continue to glean from the parable by focusing on God's mercy to us and our mercy to others. Due to the nature of today's material, you may feel challenged. Please be as honest as possible and allow the Holy Spirit to lead and guide you. He will reveal all truth to us.

Read Luke 23:33-35. How does Jesus respond to the crowds who seek to kill him?

_____

Ask the LORD to search your heart and fill in the blank with someone you need to forgive.

Father, forgive _____, for he does not know what he is doing.

So what does it mean to forgive?

- Forgiveness involves an act in which someone has wronged us. In forgiveness, we do not ignore the pain or deny the hurt. Neither do we condone the action or excuse the sin. Rather we acknowledge it and lay it at the foot of the cross.

- Forgiveness is not a feeling but an act of will in which we trust the LORD to right our wrong. We *choose* to forgive, a deliberate choice. We choose to release the offender and the offense and to no longer hold on to the pain and anger.

- Forgiveness is commanded, no matter the offense committed against us. Testimony after testimony encourages us that God's grace is sufficient to help us forgive not only every day offenses like someone cutting us off in traffic, a nagging spouse, or a bothersome co-worker but also to forgive marital infidelity, abusive parents, or the murder of a loved one.

- Forgiveness does not always relieve the consequences for the offender. For example, if someone kills my child, though I forgive him, he may still have to serve in prison for his crime.

When it comes to forgiveness, God has not asked us to do anything that he himself has not first demonstrated. While on the cross suffering excruciating pain, Jesus speaks amazing words of forgiveness: "Father, forgive them, for they do not know what they are doing" (Luke 23:34a). To the very people responsible for the agonizing pain he is enduring, he offers forgiveness for their offense. There is Jesus, in great pain and agony, making intercession for his transgressors (Isaiah 53:12). Many of us have taken to heart some of Jesus's last words before he returns to heaven (to make disciples of all nations), but how well have we ingrained in our hearts some of his last words before his death? When others hurt and injure us, do we as readily say *Father, forgive them, for they do not know what they are doing?*

Are there people who do not deserve forgiveness because of their sins? Explain.

How do Micah 7:18-19 and Ephesians 2:4 describe the Lord's mercy?

_____

Compare the cost of God forgiving you with the cost of you forgiving another person. Which is greater? Explain.

_____

The heart of forgiveness rests on our understanding of how much we have been forgiven. God has extended great mercy to us and forgiven us an immeasurable debt. We did nothing to earn or merit our forgiveness. In salvation, we came to the Lord spiritually bankrupt. Because of our sin, we deserved death and eternity in hell. But God, in his great mercy, did not give us what we deserved. Instead, he forgave us our sins and provided eternal life through the atoning work of Jesus.

Forgiveness is really a question of magnitude. Do we understand the magnitude of our own sin in God's eyes? Do we understand the magnitude of what God has forgiven us? Another person's sin against us is minor relative to our great sin against a holy God. Jesus died for us, not when we had a close relationship with him, but while we were his great enemies. As sinners, we opposed God and walked in wickedness. Yet, God forgave us once we repented and sought his forgiveness. If God could forgive us when we acted as his enemies, then certainly we can forgive others, even those who act as our enemies. An unforgiving heart demonstrates that we do not fully understand the magnitude of what we have been forgiven.

Are there people whom we feel do not warrant forgiveness because of their crimes? What about Judas, Hitler, or a murderer who violently kills a loved one? Would we be happy if God forgave these people? These are hard questions. Yet Scripture tells us that God freely forgives all people, regardless of how heinous their sins, if they repent. God forgives liars, adulterers, embezzlers, thieves, murderers, kidnappers, sexual abusers, and he forgives you and me. Abraham, for example, the father of a nation, lied repeatedly about his wife. David, a man after God's own heart, committed adultery with Bathsheba and murdered her husband to conceal their affair. Paul, who wrote a great portion of the New Testament, persecuted and killed Christians. Regardless of the offense committed against us, the LORD asks us to forgive it. In fact, God has already forgiven them if they are Christians; and if not, God will insure justice. We cannot withhold from someone what God has already given them, for the greater offense is not served against us but against God, for he is far holier than we are.[5]

Scripture vividly portrays God's mercy as tender, everlasting, great, rich, plentiful, and abundant. Second Corinthians 1:3 further describes God as the Father of mercies and compassion. It is clear that our LORD abounds in mercy. Micah 7:18 reveals that the LORD delights to show us mercy. He does not begrudgingly offer us mercy because he has to. He *delights* to show us mercy.

According to Micah 6:8, what are we to love?
　☐ Judgment　　☐ Mercy

Fill in the blanks - Matthew 5:7.
　Blessed are the _____ for they will be shown _____.

Reflect on your own mercifulness. When someone offends you, do you usually give him what he deserves or extend mercy to him?
　☐ Lean toward mercy　　　☐ Lean toward judgment

Challenge
Share a time when the LORD supplied you the grace to forgive someone who hurt you.

_____

The people of Jesus's time did not really value mercy. Both the Romans and Greeks viewed it negatively, seeing it as a flaw rather than a perfection, a weakness rather than a strength. Even the religious people of Jesus's day tended to operate more on a system of equity, returning good for good and evil for evil. But Jesus thought differently and repeatedly addressed this lack of mercy as he taught the crowds. He encouraged them and us to show mercy. Just as God showers mercy on us, he wants us to shower mercy on others. We are to *love* mercy, being tender hearted and compassionate toward one another. Do we embrace a merciful attitude toward others? Do we delight to show them what we have so graciously received? Can you imagine the witnesses we would be to the world if we demonstrated mercy rather than revenge? Can you imagine the unity we would preserve within the body of Christ if we could forgive petty injuries and offenses?

As we speak of mercy, I must issue a caution. Mercy does not mean that we do not rebuke sin and injustice. Our God is a God of truth and righteousness. Mercy does not allow us to turn a blind eye to wickedness or to condone sin. We must instead always stand firm for righteousness, speaking the truth in love.

In yesterday's parable, the king asks the first servant, "Shouldn't you have had *mercy* on your fellow servant just as I had on you?" (Matthew 18:33). Having bestowed great mercy on the servant, the king expects him to offer such abundant mercy to others. Do you also notice that although the first servant cries out for mercy for himself, he desires justice for the second servant? One of my previous pastors used to say that Christians often think, *Mercy for me, but judgment for you.* Mercy does not come naturally to us. Judgment comes far easier. But we cannot seek mercy for ourselves and judgment for our offenders. Having received such great mercy, we can afford to be generous to others.

In Matthew 5:7, Jesus says, "Blessed are the merciful, for they will be shown mercy." We must take seriously Jesus's words here. Jesus repeatedly warned against the hypocrisy that the religious people demonstrated; though they manifested many outwardly "right" deeds, they were inwardly riddled with sin and self-righteousness. They performed their good acts while neglecting love and mercy (Matthew 23:23).

Our inward attitudes matter as much as our outward actions. There is no substitute for mercy in our lives, and we cannot counterfeit it through our natural state. Only the LORD works mercy in us and through us for his glory. Take a moment to reflect on your Christian walk without the mercy of God. Could you make it? Absolutely not—we desperately need God's abundant, overflowing mercy in our lives. We desperately need for God to give us a clean slate, to wipe away all our sins and failures. This, then, is how desperately we need to wipe off others' slates against us.

Day 3: Betrayed by Blood

> Do not repay evil with evil or insult with insult, but with blessing, because to this you were called so that you may inherit a blessing.
>
> 1 Peter 3:9

These past few days, we have discussed the general aspects of forgiveness. Today, we will study an example of a man who graciously chose to forgive what seems unforgiveable. Joseph had every reason not to forgive his brothers, and yet he allowed God's mercy to flow through him. As we read about Joseph's story of forgiveness, may he serve to encourage us all!

Though we studied Genesis 37 in our *Downcast by Disappointment* chapter, please reread this chapter and allow the LORD to give you fresh insight.

What do Joseph's brothers plot? _____

Why would they perform such a terrible act? _____

Describe Joseph's feelings (Genesis 42:21). _____

Have you ever felt betrayed by a family member or a friend? Explain.

_____

For how much is Joseph sold (Genesis 37:28)?
☐ Twenty shekels   ☐ Thirty shekels   ☐ Forty shekels

Challenge
Who else is betrayed for a few coins (Matthew 26:14-16)? Can you think of some other similarities between these two men?

_____

What finally happens to Joseph (Genesis 37:23-28, 36)?

_____

As we discussed in our *Downcast by Disappointment* chapter, Joseph was one of the sons of Jacob and seventeen when Genesis 37 opens. Scripture informs us that of all his children, Jacob favored Joseph the most. In fact, he gives Joseph a beautiful, ornamental multi-colored coat. The coat, of course, creates great friction between Joseph and his brothers, which Joseph increases even more by reporting his brothers' mischievous misconduct to their father. The tension finally reaches a boiling point when Joseph relays two dreams that he has to his brothers. In these dreams, his brothers bow down to him.

While Joseph's brothers shepherd their father's flocks near Shechem, Jacob sends Joseph to check on them. From the distance, Joseph's brothers see him and plot to kill him. Reuben, the oldest, tries to intervene and help Joseph. But alas, Joseph's brothers decide to sell him into slavery. Joseph could never have envisioned the cold-hearted betrayal that awaited him. His brothers strip his clothes and mercilessly throw him into a cistern. Then they have the gall to sit down and enjoy their meal as if nothing has happened. Seeing a caravan of Midianites, the brothers decide to sell Joseph as a slave because they do not want to kill their own flesh and blood. Seems a little ironic, doesn't it? Poor Joseph, betrayed by his own flesh and blood, betrayed for a measly twenty pieces of silver. It reminds us of our LORD and how he is betrayed for only thirty pieces of silver. In fact, Joseph is often considered a prototype of Christ for his story contains many similarities to Jesus's story.

Can you imagine the thoughts and feelings of poor Joseph? Lonely, isolated, betrayed by those he loves most. Some of you can empathize with Joseph and know exactly the pain and anguish he suffers; others of us can only imagine. It is never easy when a family member or friend betrays us. But Joseph is not alone, just as we are not alone when we face betrayal. The LORD is always with us, and he sees the great pain we feel. He empathizes with us, for he too knows the excruciating sting of betrayal. After all, one of his friends, a man with whom he spent three years, betrayed him. Though Judas had enjoyed the privilege of our LORD's fellowship and had witnessed Jesus's spectacular miracles, he betrayed Jesus. I should also note that though Judas betrayed Jesus, the other disciples all denied him as well. In the face of the impending cross, Jesus's time of greatest need for support, all of the disciples failed him and left him (Matthew 26:56). Yet amazingly Jesus forgave them all.

Since we have already studied many of the other events of Joseph's life in our *Downcast by Disappointment* chapter, we will fast forward to his reconciliation with his brothers. Through God's providential hand, Joseph's brothers have come to Egypt in search of grain. They now stand before Joseph, but they do not recognize him because some twenty years have passed and Joseph now resembles an Egyptian in both looks and dress.

Recall an instance in which you were hurt and sought revenge? Did it help?

_____

Read Genesis 45:1-15 and Genesis 50:15-21. How does Joseph react to his brothers?

_____

What does Scripture say about taking revenge?

    Proverbs 17:13 _____

    Romans 12:17-21 _____

Apply 1 Peter 3:8-9 to Joseph. How does he return good for evil?

_____

Have you ever had to return good for evil? What happened?

_____

Our natural instinct is to take justice into our own hands and to avenge our wrongs. Sometimes retaliation seems the only way. But revenge and retaliation are never the answer. They will not alleviate our pain or solve our problems, only create greater problems and more issues. Though it may seem fulfilling for a moment, revenge will always leave a bitter taste in our mouths. Scripture repeatedly commands us to leave vengeance to the LORD. "Do not repay anyone evil for evil...Do not take revenge, my friends, but leave room for God's wrath, for it is written: 'It is mine to avenge; I will repay,' says the LORD" (Romans 12:17-19). This is a challenging passage, isn't it? The LORD commands us to not only abstain from evil but also to return good. Not repaying evil for evil is challenging in itself;

but then the LORD goes deeper and commands us to return good for evil. He expects us to operate on the basis of forgiveness and mercy, as we discussed on Day 2.

Joseph serves as a tremendous example to us of forgiveness and of returning good for evil. When he sees his brothers again, he forgives them and does not hold a grudge against them. Can you imagine? After all Joseph has endured because of them, he *chooses* to forgive. Notice that as soon as he reveals himself to them, he reassures them and places them at ease. He helps his brothers feel forgiven. If we seek to retain power over our offenders, we have not truly forgiven them. Notice also that Joseph does not give them a brief history of everything he has suffered because of their evil act and then say, "I forgive you." No, he allows the past to remain buried. Joseph also completes the reconciliation process in private. He excuses all the extra servants so that he can be alone with his brothers. To the extent possible, forgiveness and reconciliation should be a private matter between the offenders and us. Joseph even desires to bless his brothers, returning good for their evil. He provides them with farmland and provisions for the next five years of famine. "Make sure that nobody pays back wrong for wrong, but always try to be kind to each other and to everyone else" (1 Thessalonians 5:15).

Joseph also does not gloat over the circumstances. Years have passed, and he now possesses the upper hand. He has realized God's dreams, and his brothers have now bowed before him. Yet Joseph does not gloat over his brothers' misfortune. There are no "I told you sos." He does not rejoice in their downfall or humbling but instead acts with remarkable grace and mercy. "Do not gloat when your enemy falls; when he stumbles, do not let your heart rejoice" (Proverbs 24:17).

Day 4: A Bitter Root

> See to it that no one misses the grace of God and that no bitter root grows up to cause trouble and defile many.
>
> Hebrews 12:15

The soil of unforgiveness breeds many roots, none of which is productive or useful to our maturity as Christians. If we do not exercise caution, these roots will grow within us and will overgrow our hearts, crowding out our focus on the LORD and eliminating our abundant joy and peace.

According to Ephesians 4:30-31, of what should we rid ourselves?

_____

Fill in the blanks - Hebrews 12:15.
See to it that no one misses _____ and that _____ grows up to cause _____ and defile many.

Who does bitterness hurt? Circle all that apply.
The offender   Me   Innocent bystanders

Can you think of any areas in which you have planted a seed for bitterness by not forgiving someone?

_____

What steps should we take if we carry a grudge against someone (Mark 11:25, Matthew 5:23-24)?

_____

An unforgiving spirit can easily result in bitterness. And bitterness is no small thing. Once the seed of bitterness takes root, it produces its sour fruit. It will mar and ruin everything that is beautiful in our lives. It will imprison us by turning our gaze inward, poisoning our lives with self-pity and endangering the joy we possess. It will also sever our fellowship with the Father.

When we fail to forgive others, we hurt many people. We hurt those around us, the person we will not forgive, and many innocent bystanders who are caught in the crossfire. But we hurt ourselves the most. By permitting the grievance to continually cause us pain, we become its victim all over again. We sacrifice our freedom and joy to the vicious control of the offense.

An unforgiving spirit can also result in a critical spirit. Have you ever noticed how if we have not truly forgiven people, we become very critical of them, magnifying their faults and searching for actions which we can criticize? Bitterness distorts our view of everything. We often see what we desire to see and hear what we desire to hear, all of which serves to fuel our bitterness. For example, I remember a time when I listened to a message from someone with whom I was frustrated. I recounted what the person had said to my husband, only to later listen again to the message and realize that what I heard differed from what the person had actually said. I had heard what I had wanted to hear.

Unforgiveness also contaminates our prayer life. In Mark 11:25, Jesus instructs us to stop praying and to proactively try and reconcile with our offender. God wants us to forgive those who hurt us. In fact, if we only perceive an offense has occurred, the offender may never apologize because he does not realize he has done something wrong. We could waste precious time allowing bitterness to develop over *nothing*. We must also remember that bitterness is our sin, not the sin of our offender.

What does love cover (1 Peter 4:8)?

_____

Challenge
Read Genesis 9:18-25. How do Shem and Japheth cover their father's offense?

_____

What should we take captive (2 Corinthians 10:5)? Why?

_____

Do you tend to discuss your hurts with your friends? Does this help or hinder you in forgiving others?

_____

So how can we ensure that we do not become bitter?

- First, we must *choose to forgive*. Bitterness only develops when we refuse to forgive an offender. Sounds simple, doesn't it? Yet forgiveness is not always easy. Forgiving parents who have let us down, friends who have hurt us, or co-workers who have wronged us can seem daunting, if not impossible. But all is possible with God. We must ask him to help us forgive.

  Choosing to forgive also means that we do not broadcast our offenders' sins to other people. First Peter 4:8 reminds us to remain fervent in our love for love covers another's sins. The Greek word for fervent means to stretch out. The LORD is stretching our love for others. This does not mean that we ignore the sin or unrighteous behavior. Rather, once it has been confessed and dealt with, we do not publicize it to others, even through the guise of prayer. "He who covers over an offense promotes love" (Proverbs 17:9a). Scripture reveals a beautiful story about how two of Noah's children covered his sin (Genesis 9:18-23). Noah drinks some wine and becomes drunk, lying uncovered inside his tent. Seeing his father's nakedness, Ham exposes it by telling his brothers, Shem and Japheth. Shem and Japheth, however, cover it. They carry a garment inside the tent and cover their father with it. God does not expose our sin to other people but buries it in the deepest part of the sea. This, then, is how we must treat others' sins once they repent.

As we forgive, we must also ensure that we have not developed bitterness against God. As we face difficulties and challenges, we sometimes question God's actions. Why does he allow our precious children to die? Why do our loving mothers have Alzheimers? Why have we lost our jobs after serving faithfully for years? Eventually our questions can develop into anger, which then may lead to bitterness. Sometimes we even attribute wrongdoing to God in order to defend our positions. Yet we cannot malign the LORD because we do not like or understand his way. "Would you discredit my justice? Would you condemn me to justify yourself?" (Job 40:8).

- Second, we must forgive completely and unconditionally just as the LORD has forgiven us. "As far as the east is from the west, so far has he [the LORD] removed our transgressions from us" (Psalm 103:12). Sometimes we experience limited forgiveness in which we only partially forgive an offender. We still cling to some of the hurt and hence continue to experience negative feelings toward the person. Yet the LORD wants us to forgive *completely*.

- Third, we must control our thoughts by taking them captive, or they will wreak havoc in our minds. As soon as unforgiving or bitter thoughts enter our minds, we need to stop them and dwell on edifying thoughts instead. Our minds are battlefields, and we easily incite our bitterness toward someone by constantly replaying their offense against us. No matter how much time we spend "reviewing" an offense, it will not make the offense better or eliminate the hurt. We must also be careful how much we share with our friends. Continually talking about our hurts usually adds fuel to the fire because our friends normally sympathize with us, encouraging the hurt rather than helping us to move past it. Reviewing our hurts has a way of stirring up the bitterness and compounding the pain. We may also unknowingly magnify the wrong. Instead, we can try verbally sharing it with the LORD or even journaling our feelings.

- Fourth, we need to pray diligently. If we find that we have become bitter, then we need to turn to our LORD and ask him to set us free from its prison. We should also pray for our offender. This helps us see him with human eyes and move past the offense. When the Israelites entered captivity by the Babylonians, the LORD interestingly told them to pray for their oppressors and for the city to which they had been taken (Jeremiah 29:7). Can you imagine, the LORD asked the Israelites to pray for the people who had enslaved and oppressed them; but in doing so, the Israelites would be blessed. Like the Israelites, let us also pray for those who hurt and oppress us.

- Fifth, we need to remain submitted to the Holy Spirit. As we harbor ill feelings toward others, we grieve the Holy Spirit, breaking fellowship with our wondrous Father. This also means that we forego the blessings of God, like his joy, peace, and contentment.

Even though it is easy to succumb to bitterness because of our hurts and pains, we cannot encourage such feelings. If we allow our bitterness to envelop us, it will not be a small detour in our Christian walk. We will travel down a path we should not go, a path of self-pity, dejection, and despair. And we will remain there for longer than we could ever imagine. We also provide Satan a great foothold in our lives if we do not forgive, and we open ourselves up to other sins, like anger, lying, murder, and so forth. Instead, let's ask God to help us move past all hurts so that we can experience his joy and peace.

Day 5: Perfect Justice

> Will not the Judge of all the earth do right?
>
> Genesis 18:25b

In forgiving others, we do not condone the unrighteous or sinful acts of others. Instead, we allow God, as our protector and avenger, to administer perfect justice. We allow him to defend us amidst a world of wickedness and iniquity. We allow him to right our wrongs.

How does Genesis 16:13 refer to God?

_____

Who does the LORD watch (Proverbs 15:3)?
    ☐ The good   ☐ The wicked   ☐ Both

What will God bring into judgment (Ecclesiastes 12:14)?

_____

Does God see the pain that his people endure?

    Exodus 3:7-9 _____

    Revelation 2:8-11 _____

How does it encourage you to know that the LORD has seen every hurt and offense ever committed against you?

_____

Even when someone commits the worst act against us, Scripture tells us that we have no need to retaliate. Instead, we need to rest in the LORD and allow him to enact perfect justice. But leaving justice to the LORD is not always an easy task. Sometimes it appears that ungodly people win: criminals avert justice, the sinful rich enjoy prosperity, and offenders live a life of ease. As time passes, we may think that God has forgotten us or that he has overlooked justice. But he has not, and he sees all the hurts and offenses that others have perpetrated against us. In Scripture one of God's names is *El Roi*, the God who sees. God's "eyes" penetrate through the darkness, even to the most remote places on earth. There is nothing that God does not see. "Nothing in all creation is hidden from God's sight. Everything is uncovered and laid bare before the eyes of him to whom we must give account" (Hebrews 4:13). The Hebrew word for *laid bare* means

> To expose or lay open. The word was used of the bending back of the neck of wrestlers by their opponent. The bending back of the neck was used also on an animal to be slaughtered for an offering in order to expose the throat; hence, figuratively to lay bare or open.[6]

Everything is laid bare before God. There is nothing that we can hide. No event escapes his eyes or his judgment. God sees our pains as cruel acts are committed against us. He sees our miseries as many of life's events unfold. He sees our heartaches as friends betray us. Others may never know what we suffer or endure; they may never see the pain and hardship. But our LORD, he knows, he sees, and he comforts.

How is God described in the following verses?

Genesis 18:25b _____

Psalm 94:1-2 _____

Will God leave the guilty unpunished (Nahum 1:2-3)?
☐ Yes   ☐ No

Reclaiming Your Joy

Read Acts 7:54-60 and answer the following questions.

How does Acts 7:55 describe Stephen? _____

What is Stephen's response to his stoning? _____

Who watches Stephen's stoning? _____

Our ability to rely on God for justice rests on our understanding of his character. Scripture repeatedly affirms that God is just. He always acts rightly. "He is the Rock, his works are perfect, and all his ways are just. A faithful God who does no wrong, upright and just is he" (Deuteronomy 32:4). Because God is holy and just, he must punish sin. God cannot overlook or condone sin. It would violate his very nature. So we do not have to fear that God will overlook someone's sin against us. Because the LORD sees all things and possesses perfect knowledge, he is able to administer justice perfectly. God will always insure justice, whether in this lifetime or in eternity. He will settle all scores, and he is far better at vindicating us that we could ever be at vindicating ourselves.

So we must ask ourselves, do we really believe that God is just? Do we truly believe that he will enact perfect justice? If so, then why do we so intently pursue vengeance ourselves, taking justice into our own hands? Why do we threaten bodily harm to our enemies? Why do we gossip or talk badly about our adversaries? A desire for revenge in this earthly life will cripple us. We will squander our time, our resources, and our energy. We cannot allow ourselves to be so easily diverted from our mission by immersing ourselves in ways to "even" the score or to make our plight known. God is our great protector and our avenger; he will insure that perfect justice is attained.

As we speak of God's justice, I must stress that in our hearts we should desire mercy for our offenders, even though that is an extremely difficult thing at times. Stephen provides a beautiful example of seeking mercy for others. When the religious people hear Stephen speak of Jesus, they become enraged and seek to kill him. They drag him outside the city and stone him. As they throw stones at him, Stephen prays for his persecutors. He prays that the LORD will not hold their sin against them. Can you imagine? These people want to brutally and maliciously murder Stephen, and he seeks their forgiveness before God, even though not one of them has asked for forgiveness. What about us? Are we people who seek vengeance for our persecutors, or are we Stephens who seek reconciliation for others?

And do you notice the bystander Saul? Saul will later become known as Paul, a man devoted to the cause of Christ and who will eventually write a great portion of the New Testament. What if instead of mercy, Stephen had sought God's wrath for everyone there, including Paul? No doubt Stephen's image long stayed with Paul and impacted him tremendously in his Christian walk. In the end, Stephen dies as a man full of the Holy Spirit, as evidenced by his willingness to forgive and extend mercy.

As we end this week on unforgiveness, I want to stress that no matter what we face, God's grace will enable us to forgive those who hurt and grieve us, no matter the seriousness of the act perpetrated against us. Corrie Ten Boom provides a powerful example of a woman who allowed God's grace to flow through her to forgive the "unforgiveable."

Corrie was the youngest of four children born in Haarlem, Holland in 1892. Her family members were committed followers of Jesus Christ. After Holland surrendered to the Nazis, her family started hiding Jewish men and women. After one and a half years of hiding Jews, the Gestapo raided her family's home and arrested her father, her sister Betsie, and herself. Corrie's father died shortly after the raid from illness while Corrie and Betsie were sent to a concentration camp.

Though in a concentration camp, Corrie and Betsie remained committed to the LORD, reading their Bible and holding worship services. Months and months in the horrid concentration camp did not daunt their faith in the LORD. Finally, due to a clerical error, the Gestapo released Corrie. She went on to become an evangelist, sharing her story with others and focusing on the theme of forgiveness.

In her book *Tramp for the Lord*, Corrie wrote of an incident about forgiveness. She had just finished speaking to an audience about forgiveness when one of the cruelest guards from Ravensbruck, the concentration camp to which she had been sent, approached her. Amazingly, he had become a Christian and now asked for her forgiveness.

> And I stood there…and could not forgive. Betsie had died in that place-could he erase her slow terrible death simply for the asking?… And still I stood there with the coldness clutching my heart. But forgiveness is not an emotion - I knew that too. Forgiveness is an act of the will, and the will can function regardless of the temperature of the heart. "Jesus, help me!" I prayed silently. "I can lift my hand. I can do that much. You supply the feeling." And so woodenly, mechanically, I thrust my hand into the one stretched out to me. And as I did, an incredible thing took place. The current started in my shoulder, raced down my arm, sprang into our joined hands. And then this healing warmth seemed to flood my whole being, bringing tears to my eyes. "I forgive you, brother!" I cried. "With all my heart!" For a long moment we grasped each other's hands, the former guard and former prisoner. I had never known God's love so intensely as I did then.[7]

Corrie demonstrated the incredible forgiveness that God daily shows to us. Sometimes forgiveness seems impossible, and so we must trust our LORD. When we exhibit a willingness to forgive, God will always provide us the grace sufficient to forgive. He will meet us where we are and empower us to do that which he commands. Forgiveness is always possible if we are truly willing.

Week 7:
Troubled by Trials

Day 1: The Road to Glory

Day 2: Songs in the Night

Day 3: Sifted like Wheat

Day 4: The Sweetness of Suffering

Day 5: A Divine Appointment

Key Thoughts for the Week

Day 1:   The road to glory is strewn with hardship and suffering, yet God's joy for us is deeper than any situation we face.

Day 2:   God's primary concern for our life is not our comfort but our character.

Day 3:   God lovingly allows us to be sifted because there is chaff in our lives that needs to be removed.

Day 4:   Our suffering becomes sweet as we realize that trials are special times with our LORD, treasured moments of growth.

Day 5:   Trials are a divine appointment by God sovereignly orchestrated to help us grow and mature in our faith.

Day 1: The Road to Glory

> Dear friends, do not be surprised at the painful trial you are suffering, as though something strange were happening to you.
>
> 1 Peter 4:12

Experiencing enduring joy in our lives means learning how to deal with trials and hardships. Too often we become a captive to our circumstances and allow them to steal our joy. Trials have the uncanny habit of creating havoc with our spiritual and emotional well-being by removing our focus from the LORD, the source of our joy. So let's spend this week learning how to be overcomers, people who live joyful lives no matter what we face.

Should trials and hardships surprise us (1 Peter 4:12)?

    ☐ Yes   ☐ No

What will happen if we desire to live a godly life (2 Timothy 3:12-15)?

_____

According to Philippians 1:29-30, what two privileges have we received?

    1. _____   2. _____

Based on 2 Corinthians 6:4-5 and 11:23-28, describe some of Paul's hardships.

_____

Assess some of your expectations of the Christian walk. Do you think it will be easy? Do you expect to have to suffer? Do you expect your walk could be like Paul's?

_____

One of the main stumbling blocks to joy during trials is unrealistic expectations. Many Christians do not expect challenges and difficulties. They believe everything will occur smoothly once they accept Jesus as LORD and Savior, living under the false assumption that the Christian walk will be easy and comfortable. Yet Scripture repeatedly informs us that we will experience trials and hardship. Trials are not some strange or alien events that occur in our lives; they are inevitable parts of our Christian walk, the norm, not the anomaly. Sometimes we "know" that the Christian walk entails trials, and yet we still expect to escape such hardships. We rationalize that other Christians may face difficulties but not us; the LORD will somehow keep us from such hardships. Though we may "know" that the Christian walk entails suffering, it still has not penetrated into our inner sanctums, or we would not so easily question and doubt God as soon as adversity strikes.

Philippians 1:29 reminds us that we have received two privileges: to believe on Christ and to suffer for his name. "For it has been granted to you on behalf of Christ not only to believe on him, but also to suffer for him" (Philippians 1:29). The Greek word translated *granted* is *charizomai* and means "to show someone a favor, be kind to. To give or bestow a thing willingly."[1] It is a privilege, a gift from the LORD. Many of us willingly accept God's gracious gift of salvation, but do we as willingly accept his gift of *suffering*? But we cannot divorce the two blessings. As we speak of the Christian walk, we tend to shy away from the topic of suffering because it is not an easy topic. Who of us wants to incur pain for Christ's sake or be persecuted for our faith? Yet we do a great disservice to ourselves if we do not understand suffering and trials and their relation to our Christian walk. The road to glory is paved with rocks. Some hardships are only pebbles, others are giant boulders. Some stand alone, others are clustered together. But make no mistake about it, our paths are littered with many different trials: the dismissal from a job we love, the rejection of a friend, the loss of a child, the abandonment of a spouse, the loss of health, the ridicule of a co-worker, and the list goes on. If we want to remain joyous during trials, we must dispel the myth that we will have comfortable paths devoid of any rocks. We will not. The path to glory is strewn with the rocks of hardship and suffering.

Paul serves as a beautiful example of a godly man who faithfully followed the LORD and yet endured great hardships. In his letter to the Corinthians, Paul elaborates on some of this suffering and hardship: he was thrown into prison repeatedly, beaten and flogged many times, exposed to death frequently, shipwrecked, survived on the open sea, went without food and clothes, felt cold and lonely. He also faced danger from his own countrymen, the Gentiles, and false brothers. Forsaken, rejected, and alone—is this what we realistically expect may happen in our Christian walk? Or do we somehow expect an easy, comfortable life as we glide into heaven?

Does righteous behavior always receive a positive *earthly* reward? Explain.

_____

Challenge
How are Daniel (Daniel 6:7-16) and Shadrach, Meschach, and Abednego (Daniel 3:12-20) rewarded for their righteous behavior?

_____

Read John 15:18-21 about the Christian's interaction in the world and answer the following questions.

What warning does Jesus give us? _____

Why does the world system hate Christians? _____

What is the progression of the world's feelings toward Christians?

John 15:18-19 _____ John 15:20 _____ John 16:2 _____

In John 15:18-21, Jesus warns us that the world will hate us. Why does the world hate us? Because we do not belong to the world but to our LORD, and we seek to make known his glory. As Christians, we possess different value systems, attitudes, and beliefs than the world. Inherently righteousness challenges unrighteousness, and purity confronts wickedness. Most of the world refuses to acknowledge its sin and repent before the LORD; hence a friction is created. Not all people, including Christians, want their sins confronted. Remember, Jesus embodied purity, truth, kindness, light, and love, and yet sinful people crucified him. Please understand that I am not saying that our righteous actions will always receive a negative response; but they certainly can, and we need to remain prepared for that. Our righteous behavior can easily have an earthly cost, like being fired for not changing our company's financial numbers or being excluded because we refuse to gossip with friends. Not everyone appreciates having someone act righteously around him. It can be very discouraging if we are not prepared for others to respond negatively to us. We rarely consider that our Christian walk may entail sacrifice and loneliness, even within Christian circles.

Do you notice the progression in the world's opposition to us, as Christians? First, the world hates us. Then it seeks to persecute us, and finally it seeks to kill us. The stronger we grow in our identification with Christ, the greater the threat we become to the world. How popular are we in the world? Are we getting along with the world, or do we stand as a reproach to it? If we are truly living for Christ, we will not be very popular in this world. We may not experience physical persecution but may instead be mocked or excluded from social events. If we are always getting along with the world, then something may be wrong. Perhaps at work we have remained silent when godliness required us to speak up for truth even if it meant being fired? Perhaps we have hidden in the shadows when godliness required us to step out into the light and become a target? Perhaps we have followed the Christian masses to ensure popularity, when godliness required us to take a different course of action? The world hated our LORD, and if we identify with him, it will hate us as well. A servant is not greater than his master. Let us stand for our LORD, regardless of the cost. These are the defining moments of our faith.

The leader of this world is Satan (1 John 5:19, 2 Corinthians 4:4). And more than anything, Satan seeks our demise. Sometimes we forget that we are in a spiritual war. And yet every day, a spiritual war rages around us for the souls of men. It is so easy to forget that this world is a battlefield, especially as we live in our comfortable homes, go to work everyday, shuttle our children to activities, and continue our daily routines. We focus on the physical realities while forgetting the spiritual realm. Satan, our great opponent, however, never forgets, and he seeks to damage and destroy everything that is godly. As we grow closer to our LORD and perform work that glorifies him, Satan will oppose us. He will create division, strife, and unexpected problems. We cannot remain naive and uninformed. We must expect opposition to godly endeavors.

It is important that we possess a realistic view of the Christian walk, otherwise trials and suffering will devastate us. We will become discouraged and disheartened. We may even accuse God of wrongdoing or unfaithfulness. Satan's voice seems so enticing as he whispers that the LORD does not love us or he would not allow us to suffer so much.

As we assess our Christian walk, it can easily seem overwhelming. Briefly studying Paul's hardships and our current spiritual war could completely discourage us and make us want to run for the hills, so let's keep a proper perspective. There is no doubt that the Christian walk entails trials and hardships, but God's joy for us is deeper than any situation we face. Whatever trial we experience is more than compensated by his magnificent presence. "You have made known to me the path of life; you will fill me with joy in your presence, with eternal pleasures at your right hand" (Psalm 16:11).

Day 2: Songs in the Night

> About midnight Paul and Silas were praying and singing hymns to God, and the other prisoners were listening to them.
>
> Acts 16:25

Yesterday, I said that God's joy for us is deeper than any situation that we face. But is this true? Can God's joy really hold us in the midst of extreme pain and suffering? And what if we are imprisoned or tortured is God's joy still deeper than our situation? Though it seems impossible, God's joy is indeed greater than any hardship we experience and any trial we face. Today, our study of Paul and Silas will reveal how deep God's joy for us truly is.

Read Acts 16:16-25. What happens to Paul and Silas? What is their response?

_____

Challenge

Read Acts 5:40-42. How do the apostles leave the Sanhedrin? Do you notice a recurring theme concerning the apostles' response to trials and suffering?

_____

Read Psalm 126:5-6. What encouragement do you receive from these verses?

_____

After performing the LORD's work and healing a demonized girl, Paul and Silas encounter great opposition from the girl's owners since they have lost a source of income. The girl's owners incite the magistrates (Roman officers) who order Paul and Silas to be beaten and thrown into prison. Take a moment to absorb the gravity of what is happening. Paul and Silas have done nothing wrong, only performed the LORD's work, and yet their "reward" is to be beaten and imprisoned in an inner cell. They do not even have the opportunity to defend their actions. As we discussed yesterday, the earthly "reward" for our righteous behavior is not always what we might expect. So there are Paul and Silas in a dark, cold, smelly cell with their bodies aching from pain, their backs bloodied from their beating, and their feet placed in stocks. It would have been easy to succumb to despair, feel forsaken by the LORD, or to complain. Yet, Paul and Silas never succumb to despair or wallow in the injustice of their situation. They choose instead to confidently trust in their LORD, praying and singing hymns to him. What is our reaction when adversity strikes? Is prayer our first refuge? Is praise? It is in these difficult times that the LORD gives us songs in the night, but we cannot remain so focused on ourselves or our dismal circumstances that we miss them. Charles Spurgeon, the famous preacher who lived in the nineteenth century, commented,

> Any fool can sing in the day. It is easy to sing when we can read the notes by daylight; but the skillful singer is he who can sing when there is not a ray of light to read by…Songs in the night come only from God; they are not in the power of men.[2]

Paul's joy seems almost unreal, doesn't it? And yet Paul will not allow his circumstances to dictate his level of joy. Even if he loses every material possession and every physical comfort, he still has his LORD and salvation. Please note that it is not that our trials are easy, for they are not. Most trials are difficult and burdensome.

Instead, we experience God's joy during them. We cannot succumb to Satan's deceitful whispers that our joy depends on our circumstances. It does not; it depends on our relationship with the LORD. Even in the most trying of times, in the greatest of adversity, the LORD can enable us to experience the deepest levels of joy. Do you doubt me? Read again this passage on Paul and Silas. Even adversity and hardship could not dull Paul's joy.

Read Acts 16:25-34. How does Paul and Silas's behavior impact those around them?

_____

A joyful witness can often help the cause of Christ while a joyless witness can hinder it. In this past week, did your witness help or hinder the cause of Christ?

_____

The LORD answers Paul and Silas's prayers in a dramatic way, for their cell door flies open and their chains are unfastened. Paul and Silas could easily have escaped with no thought for anyone else, but Paul and Silas are no ordinary prisoners. They are men on a mission for their LORD, servants of the Most High. So they stay in the prison and share the gospel with the jailer. At that moment, the jailer falls face down, having witnessed the power within these men. Paul, now in a position of authority, could easily have abused his power or walked away, rationalizing his behavior by telling himself that the jailer would deserve what he received. After all, staying in the prison could mean his recapture and re-imprisonment, perhaps even death. Paul and Silas give little thought to their own lives and seek instead to help the jailer. And in the end, the jailer and his whole family are saved.

In the meanwhile, I assume, though Scripture does not explicitly say, that the other prisoners are astounded by what they see. It is probably unbelievable to the other prisoners that these men could be in these horrible circumstances and yet pray and sing hymns. Can you picture Paul and Silas's joyful voices echoing through the dark, cold prison walls? If that does not shock the prisoners, then I am sure they are stunned by the fact that Paul and Silas have the opportunity to escape and yet delay it to help their own jailer. Radical, isn't it? It would be hard to witness Paul and Silas's amazing joy and their concern for the jailer and not be moved by it.

Most people can remain happy when things go well, but it is when adversity strikes that Christians have the true opportunity to shine. It is during these times that Christians can offer something that the world cannot, a joy that is unreal. Trials, more than any other times, are the moments when non-Christians see that Christians possess something greater than what is found in this earthly world. They witness a joy that abounds no matter the hardships and struggles of this world.

Read James 1:2-4 and 1 Peter 1:6-9. Why can we consider our trials "pure joy"?

_____

According to 2 Corinthians 3:18, how are we being transformed?
    From _____ to _____

Recall a trial that you have recently faced. Did you rejoice during the trial—why or why not?

_____

In the first chapter of James, James makes a startling statement to the Jerusalem Christians. He instructs them to consider it "pure joy" when they face trials. At the time, the Jerusalem church was undergoing severe persecution and hardships; thus it would seem revolutionary for James to command these Christians to consider such trials "pure joy." And yet James's command seems to resonate through the pages of Scripture. Peter also encourages Christians to rejoice in their hardships and sufferings. "But rejoice that you participate in the sufferings of Christ, so that you may be overjoyed when his glory is revealed" (1 Peter 4:13). The Greek word *agalliao*, translated *overjoyed*, means "to exult, leap for joy, to show one's joy by leaping and skipping denoting excessive or ecstatic joy and delight."[3] And Paul clearly tells the Philippians, "Rejoice in the LORD always. I will say it again: Rejoice!" (Philippians 4:4).

So how can we rejoice during difficult times that completely overwhelm us?

1. *We rejoice because trials prove our relationship to the Lord.*

Trials reveal our bond and fellowship with God. If we never experience difficulties and hardships, we should wonder whether we are truly children of God for God has ordained that *all* of his children undergo trials and testing. Trials and testing prove the genuineness of our faith.

2. *We rejoice because we know that trials develop our character.*

We can rejoice in our trials because we know that the LORD is developing our character and maturing our faith. "Not only so, but we also rejoice in our sufferings, because we know that suffering produces perseverance; perseverance, character; and character, hope" (Romans 5:3-4). The LORD uses trials to build our character, refine our dispositions, and spur on our maturity. There are no short cuts to spirituality. There are some things that can only be learned during the valley of suffering and the crucible of hardship. We must also remember that the LORD's primary concern for our lives is not our comfort but rather our character. Most times what we choose for ourselves is rarely good for our character. We tend to choose comfortable, easy options, but those choices rarely create spiritual muscle in us. They do not stretch and challenge us. With the precision of a surgeon, the LORD uses trials to remove sin and ungodly habits and to cultivate character and maturity. Second Corinthians 3:18 reminds us that we are being transformed from glory to glory. How exciting! How worth all the pain and suffering we endure in this earthly life. God does not have to change the circumstances in order for us to be joyful; he need only change us.

One of the greatest needs of today is for us to cultivate our character and to mature in the LORD. Though as new Christians we started out in the shallow end of the pool, we must stop playing there and move into the deep end. All the real fun and adventure are found in God's deep oceans, not in the kiddie pools.

Day 3: Sifted like Wheat

> Simon, Simon, Satan has asked to sift you as wheat.
>
> Luke 22:31

Yesterday, we briefly discussed how we can rejoice in our trials because we know that the LORD is developing our character. Let's delve a little deeper into this area by discussing the sifting of Peter and how this developed his character and allowed him to mature.

Read Luke 22:31-34. How does Peter respond to Jesus's warning?

_____

What else partly contributes to Peter's fall (Matthew 26:31-45)?

_____

What warning do we receive from 1 Corinthians 10:11-12? Are there areas in your life in which you think Satan could never succeed in his attack on you?

_____

Jesus's time of crucifixion has almost arrived, and while enjoying some of his last moments with the disciples, Jesus utters those ominous words to Simon Peter, "Simon, Simon, Satan has asked to sift you as wheat" (Luke 22:31). Interestingly, in the Greek, the word *you* is in the plural, implying that Satan has asked to sift all the disciples. Sifting involves a process in which grain is fiercely shaken to separate the chaff from the wheat. Jesus is gently warning Peter that he is about to be sifted. Jesus also says that he has prayed for Peter. What great comfort to know that as the LORD sends us into the fire, he lovingly prays for us.

Peter, in his typical headstrong and impetuous manner, discounts the LORD's warning. With his normal passion, he avows his devotion to the LORD and affirms his willingness to go to prison and even die for the LORD. One would think that with God in front of him, Peter would have taken greater heed of the master's warning; but alas, Peter is headstrong, independent, and feeling infallible. Like Peter, we must be careful not to ignore our LORD's cautions.

Peter goes even further and boasts that if all the disciples stumble, he never will. We receive a little glimpse here of Peter's pride. He thinks he is probably better than the other disciples—they might stumble, but he never will. Sometimes we may feel invincible and superior to other people in certain areas; as a result, we can become overly confident in ourselves and fail to depend on our LORD for his strength and power. We may also fail to realize that perhaps we have never sinned greatly in an area because the LORD has not yet lowered our guards and allowed Satan to truly attack us.

Presumption creates a grave danger for all of us. If we fail to realize our frailties and weaknesses, then we will not remain alert and on guard. In his boastfulness, Peter forgets his propensity to sin and the attractiveness of Satan's schemes. Sometimes, we experience trials, and instead of remaining alert and on guard, we act nonchalant and cavalier. As a result, we become easy prey for Satan and fall into his snare. "Be self-controlled and alert. Your enemy the devil prowls around like a roaring lion looking for someone to devour" (1 Peter 5:8-9). We are wise to remember how cunning Satan truly is and how easily we can be seduced by his schemes. Sometimes, we think, *I would never do that,* but few of us truly know the depth of the sin we could commit. Satan's temptations come far too prettily packaged. If Peter, who repeatedly demonstrated devotion and love for Christ, could be so sifted, then so can we. After all, Peter is not a weak, lukewarm Christian. He is a disciple who has repeatedly avowed and demonstrated devotion to Christ. Upon hearing Jesus's call, he left everything to follow Jesus (Matthew 4). For three years, he devotedly remained with Jesus. His track record is probably better than most of ours, and yet in his presumption and pride, he fails. Let Peter serve as a strong warning to any of us who proudly think we could never stumble, and let us cling to our LORD. "So, if you think you are standing firm, be careful that you don't fall!" (1 Corinthians 10:12).

It is interesting that Peter fails in an area that is his strength—his courage and devotion to the LORD. He becomes overly confident in his strength, and ultimately his strength leads to his downfall. Oswald Chambers insightfully remarked, "Unguarded strength is double weakness…The Bible characters fell on their strong points, never on their weak ones."[4] Abraham, for example, exhibited great faith by offering up his son Isaac, and yet that same faith faltered when he traveled to Egypt and he lied about Sarah. What a warning to us that we should not become overly confident in our strengths for they can easily result in our downfall.

Jesus's warning should have spurred Peter and the disciples to their knees to diligently pray for strength and courage. Jesus even warns them again in the Garden of Gethsemane to "keep watching and praying." Instead, Peter and the other disciples fall asleep. Three times Jesus rebukes them for falling asleep, and yet it produces no change in their actions—they keep falling asleep, oblivious to the danger.

Read Matthew 26:69-75. What do you notice about Peter's denial?

_____

According to Mark 14:30, how many times does the rooster crow?
  ☐ Two times   ☐ Three times

What happens after Peter third's denial (Luke 22:60-62)?

_____

Why does Jesus allow Satan to sift Peter? Why does Jesus allow Satan to sift us?

_____

Can you think of some chaff in your life, like greed, materialism, pride, gossip, envy that needs to be removed?

_____

Fast-forward a few hours: the Roman guards capture Jesus from the Garden of Gethsemane and deliver him to Annas, the former high priest's house. Meanwhile, Peter waits outside in the courtyard, warming himself before the fire. A servant, who recognizes Peter, inquires if he was with Jesus. Peter denies any involvement and moves to the gateway to avoid further questioning. Another girl, however, sees Peter and also claims that he was with Jesus. Again, Peter denies any association with Jesus, even muttering an oath. About an hour later, those near Peter once again approach him, adamantly insisting that he is with Jesus. For the third time,

Peter denies Jesus, calling down curses and swearing. Do you notice how Peter's reaction changes from a simple denial to an avowed declaration with cursing and swearing?

Not once, not twice, but three times, Peter denies his LORD. Three times he has the opportunity to stand for the LORD, and three times he chooses to remain silent. My heart breaks for Peter, and for myself at the same time. How easily Satan seduces us. How easily we all avow devotion to the LORD in one moment only to deny him before friends, neighbors, and co-workers in the next moment.

As the rooster crows, Peter remembers his LORD's words and is overcome by sadness and grief. Luke provides an additional insight: the LORD looks straight at Peter (Luke 22:61). As Peter remains in the courtyard, Jesus is in the high priest's house being interrogated. The Gospel of Mark informs us that Jesus was beaten, blindfolded, and spit upon prior to Peter's denial, so as Jesus looks at Peter, it is in his beaten and bloodied state. The Greek word translated *look* is *emblepo* and means "to look in the face, fix the eyes upon, stare at."[5] Imagine the sorrow that would overcome you as you witness your LORD bruised and beaten, knowing that you have just denied him and seeing him stare at you. The disciple, who had once declared such great devotion to his LORD, now retreats downcast and disheartened.

So why does God allow Peter to be sifted? Why does God allow us to be sifted? Why doesn't God say no to Satan and protect his faithful servant? Perhaps it is because God needs to remove some of the chaff from Peter. God allows trials in our lives for the same reason. There is chaff in our lives, sins like lying, gossip, greed, materialism, selfishness, pride, envy, and so forth, that needs to be removed.

It is vital that we also understand that the LORD lovingly allows us to undergo siftings for our good because otherwise we will doubt his love as soon as we experience trials. We will think, *If he really loved me, he would not have allowed me to lose my job. If he really loved me, he would have removed this pain.* But as we discussed in our *Downcast by Disappointment* chapter, God possesses great love for us. We are his treasured possessions. We must never doubt God's great love for us. What he does, he always does for our good. We just cannot always understand it.

Peter's failed courage does not result in his complete failure, for he quickly returns to the LORD and repents. If we allow him, God will bring good out of our worst failures. We cannot let Satan use our past failures to hinder our future. God has a purpose in every-thing. Months later, Peter will stand boldly before the Sanhedrin and preach the gospel. Perhaps God needed to allow Peter to fall so dramatically so that he would better understand the stakes and stand firmly in the more important moment. There are an endless number of reasons why God allows Peter to be sifted, and the same holds true for us. Through it all we must remember that God is good and loves us; thus he would not allow our sifting unless there was something in our lives that absolutely needed to be sifted. And we will emerge from our sifting refined and beautiful!

Day 4: The Sweetness of Suffering

> I consider that our present sufferings are not worth comparing with the glory that will be revealed in us.
>
> Romans 8:18

In the past few days, we have been discussing some of the reasons why we can remain joyous during trials and hardships: trials prove that we are children of the LORD and trials develop and mature our character. Today, we will explore some additional reasons.

Read Habakkuk 3:16-19 about a coming trial for the Israelites. How does Habakkuk respond to the situation?

What do we learn about God's presence from Psalm 139:7-12?

Challenge

What encouragement do you receive from Psalm 13:5-6, Psalm 46:1-2, and Isaiah 43:1-3?

As discussed earlier this week, we can rejoice during our trials for several reasons.

1. *We rejoice because trials prove our relationship to the Lord (Day 2).*

2. *We rejoice because we know that trials develop our character (Days 2, 3).*

3. *We also rejoice because we know that God is always with us no matter what we endure.*

God is omnipresent, which means that he is present everywhere simultaneously. Since God is omnipresent, no matter where we are, God is with us. He is with us through the joys of life and the hardships. His presence is there to reassure, comfort, and encourage us. Habakkuk understands this great truth and thus makes his powerful declaration:

> Though the fig tree does not bud and there are no grapes on the vines, though the olive crop fails and the fields produce no food, though there are no sheep in the pen and no cattle in the stalls, yet I will rejoice in the LORD, I will be joyful in God my Savior.
>
> Habakkuk 3:17-18

God has judged the Israelites' lack of faithfulness, and soon Babylon will destroy her lands, pillage the people, and ruthlessly slaughter the innocents. Knowing of the impending judgment, Habakkuk steadfastly declares his trust in the LORD and his willingness to rejoice in him.

Habakkuk learned what some of us still struggle with—that even if we lose every earthly thing, we still have our LORD and salvation. It is our relationship with our LORD that brings true inexpressible joy, not the circumstances of this world. Though trials may steal our money, our health, and our possessions, they can never steal our relationship with the LORD or our salvation; hence, we can rejoice no matter what hardship we face. God's presence can help us in any situation and can help compensate any loss we face.

4. *We rejoice because trials enable us to know God more fully.*
We rejoice in our trials because we know that our trials bring us closer to the LORD. They enable us to know him more fully, and isn't that truly the goal of our life—to know and love the LORD more each day? It is in the darkest moments of our life that we cling to the LORD the most; hence, he reveals himself to us the most, perhaps because he has our undivided attention. In *The Problem of Pain*, C. S. Lewis comments, "God whispers to us in our pleasures, speaks in our conscience, but shouts in our pains; it is his megaphone to rouse a deaf world."[6] Our trials enable us to gain a clearer view of who God is. We all have our own predisposed views of God, based on our ideas, backgrounds, and preferences. Yet we need to learn who God truly is, not who we think he is based on our preconceived ideas. It is vital that we truly know God, not just know about God. We need to experience him personally and claim him as our own. Difficulties and hardships serve as great opportunities to know God, to grow in our love for him, and to stand in awe of his magnificence.

Read Romans 8:16-18 and fill in the blanks.

I consider that our _____ are not worth comparing with the _____ that will be _____.

What encouragement do you receive from 2 Corinthians 4:16-18?

_____

Read Acts 20:17-24. How does Paul demonstrate a focus on eternity?

_____

As adversity strikes, do you notice your focus on the LORD and on eternity slipping? Explain.

_____

5.   *We rejoice because we know that our trials will provide an eternal harvest for us.*

The life we currently live will be gone in the blink of an eye, and yet all of eternity will reflect the choices that we have made. We must remain focused on our LORD and on eternity and not allow any temporary discomfort or pain to sidetrack us from our eternal goal. I am in no way making light of some of the trials and hardships that we face, but I am saying that God can use every moment of hardship that we endure to bring a greater benefit in heaven. We must cling to the promises of eternity and not allow the circumstances of today to rob us of our joy. Whatever we endure in this short, fleeting lifetime is more than compensated for in eternity.

Scripture is replete with examples of men and women who suffered a temporary, minor loss in order to secure a great, eternal reward. The early Christians, for example, joyfully accepted the seizure of their property (Hebrews 10:34). How many of us would joyfully accept the government coming in and seizing all our belongings? Yet these Christians understood that an earthly loss was temporary; an eternal reward would more than compensate for it. Trials have a tendency to disorient us and remove our focus from the LORD and from eternity, but we must re-direct our focus and place things in perspective of eternity, for eternity will reveal the true rewards of this life. The world considered Noah a fool, but eternity will reveal his faith. The world thought Stephen had been deceived because he believed in Jesus, but eternity will prove the value of his faith. And of course the world considered Jesus the greatest failure, a criminal who was crucified as a common thief; but eternity will demonstrate his greatness as everyone bows before him. We must be willing to wait until eternity, for it will reveal the greatness of our walk and faith. It is all about perspective—deferred gratification versus instant gratification. Sometimes we are swept away in the storm of suffering because it is visible and seen. It is hard for us to fully envision the glory that will be revealed in us and to understand its greatness relative to what we suffer now. And yet we must learn to place our earthly trials in perspective with our eternal glory. Our suffering is passing and temporary while the glory that will be revealed in us is heavenly and eternal. In Romans 8:18, Paul says, "I consider that our present sufferings are not worth comparing with the glory that will be revealed in us." The Greek word *logizomai*, translated *consider*, involves a numerical study or calculation. Paul is saying that if we make a detailed calculation the sum total of our suffering will be incomparable to the glory that will one day be revealed in us. Imagine a scale in which our eternal glory is contrasted with all the hardships and suffering we have endured, like the loss of a job, the rejection by a friend, or the death of a loved one. Now personalize the scale by using your own experiences.

Exercise

_____

_____

_____   Eternal glory

_____

It is hard to even picture such a scale for our eternal glory so far outweighs all our temporary trials and suffering. Remember, the eternal is always more important than the earthly.

We need to choose joy. Each one of us will face trials, but how we respond depends on us. It does *not* depend on the nature of the trial. It does *not* depend on other people and how they treat us. It does *not* depend on our circumstances. It depends on us. We choose whether we will become disillusioned and despondent or remain faithful and trusting, whether we will draw ourselves into our LORD's sweet embrace or distance ourselves from him in defiance. We choose whether we will view our trials as bitter or sweet. If we choose to view our trials as bitter, then we will miss God's best for us. There are some things that we will only learn in the valley of suffering. And rather than being impediments, these valleys are special times with our LORD, treasured moments of growth. Have you experienced the sweetness of suffering or are you still trying to swallow the bitterness of your trial? "The joy of the LORD is our strength" (Nehemiah 8:10b).

Day 5: A Divine Appointment

> So that no one would be unsettled by these trials. You know
> quite well that we were destined for them [trials].
>
> 1 Thessalonians 3:3

The degree of joy that we experience during a trial rests greatly
on our understanding of the LORD's sovereignty. God's sovereignty
is one of the most comforting doctrines that exists for us as
Christians, providing us tremendous refuge and shelter from the
difficult challenges and adversities that we face.

How do 2 Chronicles 20:6 and Daniel 4:34-35 describe God's
sovereignty?

_____

Share about a time in which God sovereignly worked out events for
your good.

_____

When we say that God is sovereign, we mean that he rules supremely
and completely, unhindered by anyone or anything. He is The Most
High and has the freedom to act as he pleases. "The LORD does
whatever pleases him, in the heavens and on the earth, in the seas
and all their depths" (Psalm 135:6). God answers to no one, explains
himself to no one, and is influenced by no one. He is autonomous,
superior, and in complete control. "For I am God, and there is no
other" (Isaiah 45:22b).

Since God is sovereign, he possesses complete control over the
events and actions that occur. There is nothing that surprises God.
He is always in control and permits certain events for his purposes.

No matter what happens, God is always on his throne and ruling magnificently.

Read Philippians 1:12-20. Describe Paul's attitude toward his imprisonment.

_____

Read Acts 12:1-11. Compare what happens to James to what happens to Peter. How do you witness God's sovereignty in this situation?

_____

Philippians 1 reveals Paul's complete trust in God's sovereignty. As the book of Philippians opens, Paul sits in prison awaiting a verdict which will either permit his release or sanction his death. The Roman method of imprisonment often included chaining a prisoner to a Roman soldier twenty-four hours a day. So Paul has lost all freedom and privacy, probably chained to a Roman guard every moment of the day. Compounding the situation, Paul's opponents are rejoicing that he is imprisoned. Rather than allowing this to discourage him, Paul joyously rests in God's sovereignty, knowing that God will work everything out for his deliverance (Philippians 1:18b-19). Paul does not complain about the circumstances, wallow in self-pity, or become bitter toward his situation. Instead, he allows his circumstances to help advance the kingdom of God. In the end, Paul's imprisonment acts as a catalyst to encourage other Christians to more boldly share the gospel.

It is interesting that Paul wears chains, yet his chains never bind him. He is far freer than some of us who have never been in physical chains. Every trial we face has the possibility of binding and crippling us. We can easily succumb to self pity, wallow in the mire of doubt, or succumb to destructive thoughts. If we truly embrace God's sovereignty, we leave no room for negative thoughts and self-pity. Remember, God has lovingly and divinely orchestrated our trials in order to create character in our lives. Thus, we do not need to negatively question his actions or lack thereof. Why is the LORD allowing this to happen? Why do I have such little money when that person is rich? Why do I have bad health when that Christian is healthy? Why? Why? Why? If we truly understand that the LORD is sovereign, we know that if the LORD wanted to give us money, he would. If he wanted to restore our health, he would. If he has chosen not to provide for us in some way, it is because those things are not consistent with his eternal goals for us. Watchman Nee was a Chinese pastor who was imprisoned for years for his dedication and commitment to Christ. He remarked that his imprisonment was not a punishment but merely a platform to advance the gospel. Watchman Nee had learned to cling to God's sovereignty and rest in his goodness. We need to radically change the way we view circumstances if we desire to remain joyous.

As God sovereignly acts, he makes wise choices. He always chooses the right option in any given situation, focusing on the eternal and not the earthly. There are many things that we will not understand in this life, and the whys will drive us crazy if we dwell on them. God is infinite and sometimes acts in ways that are inconceivable to us, ways that are consistent with his eternal goals. Just as we tell our children that they will one day understand what we are doing, so will we one day understand what our loving Father has done. In Acts 12, for example, we learn that King Herod arrests and kills the apostle James. Seeing the crowd's positive reaction to James's death, King Herod then imprisons Peter. God, however, miraculously delivers Peter. Why does the LORD preserve Peter's life but allow James to die? Does God love one apostle more than the other? No, God does not love one apostle more than the other, nor does one serve better than the other. God simply chooses to glorify himself differently through both of them. We will drive ourselves insane with the senseless why questions. There will always be questions that we cannot answer. That is why we walk by faith and not by sight.

According to 1 Thessalonians 3:2-5, for what are we destined?

_____

_____

Are God's plans ever thwarted (Isaiah 46:9-11)?
   ☐ Yes   ☐ No

Fill in the blanks - Romans 8:28.
   And we know that in _____ things God works for the _____ of those who _____, who have been called _____.

How can knowing that God's plans are never thwarted encourage you to remain joyful during a trial?

_____

_____

First Thessalonians 3:3 reminds us that we should not be disturbed by our trials because we are destined for them. The word *destined* comes from a Greek work *keimai*, and means "appointed." Our trials are appointments from God. They do not happen by chance or coincidence. They are not the result of unknown circumstances They are divine appointments from our loving Father who seeks to grow and mature us.

   Resting in God's sovereignty allows us to remain joyful as we experience the trials of this life for several reasons. First, we realize that there is nothing God could not affect if he so chooses. Since God possesses all power in heaven and earth, no one and nothing can hinder his will from being accomplished. "I know that you can do all things; no plan of yours can be thwarted" (Job 42:2). When God permits certain events to happen, it is for his purposes and plans. Thus, even in the darkest of situations, God could affect a change if he so desired. If he has not affected such a change, then we rest assured in knowing it is not for our ultimate good or for his glory.

Second, we take great solace in knowing that God does not allow our trials to exist into perpetuity. In his sovereignty, God has established clear boundaries and placed limits on what we will endure. Our hardships, no matter how difficult and taxing, are only for a season of time. He has also lovingly determined the depth of the trial we will face, promising that he will never place a trial before us that we cannot bear without his help.

Third, God promises to work everything out for our good, no matter the situation, if we love him. "And we know that in all things God works for the good of those who love him, who have been called according to his purpose" (Romans 8:28). Because Romans 8:28 provides such great encouragement to us, let's examine it a little closer.

- God promises to work out *all* things, not some things, not a few things, but all things, for the good of those who love him. God will bring good from the loss of a job, from the hurt of a friend, from the sickness of a spouse, from the disability of a child, from the loss of finances, from the mocking of others, from all things. In all circumstances, in all situations, in all trials, in all hardships, in all valleys, in all pits, God will bring good if we love him.

- Not only does God work out all things, but he does so for our *good* and *benefit*. As we speak of God bringing good out of situations, we are not saying that what has happened to us is good. For example, if someone assaults us, the action is not good, but God will bring good out of the result. Remember also that the good is from an eternal perspective, not an earthly perspective.

- In Romans 8:28, the words *work together* come from one Greek word, *sunergeo*. Our English word syneryg is derived from it. According to The New Oxford American Dictionary, synergy means "the interaction or cooperation of two or more organizations, substances, or other agents to produce a combined effect greater than the sum of their separate effects."[7] God takes our trials and produces an effect far greater than what we could ever imagine. Though one trial may seem isolated to us, God sees it in relation to the rest of our lives. Just imagine that God is painting a beautiful picture. As he completes certain parts, they may look random and scattered. But over time, he paints more spots and blends the colors to complete his masterpiece. As we look, however, we only see ink spots and chaos, but we must never forget that the artist has the full picture. We are each unique masterpieces hand crafted by the Lord. Though we cannot understand the purpose of the trials we face, our Lord, the great artist, knows exactly what he is doing. He is taking the isolated events of our lives and blending them into a great masterpiece. We have to trust him to finish the painting, and then we will stand amazed at the beautiful product.

We can take refuge in knowing that God sovereignly orchestrates our trials, places limits on their duration, and will bring good out of them. We can rejoice because we know that the hardships we endure enable us to know and love God more. Even those situations which seem the most challenging now will prove to be blessings later.

PART III:
Enduring Joy

Week 8:
Abounding in Thankfulness

Day 1: The Jewel of Joy

Day 2: Crippled by Complaining

Day 3: Praising God's Goodness

Day 4: Making Memorials

Day 5: The Garment of Salvation

Key Thoughts for the Week

Day 1:   Thankfulness magnifies our joy as we reflect on God's goodness to us.

Day 2:   Complaining and criticizing often stem from a sense of entitlement, in which we feel that we deserve better or are entitled to certain privileges.

Day 3:   Realizing that God did not have to make us, but willingly chose to do so and that he rejoices over us should create great joy and thankfulness in us.

Day 4:   Creating memorials in our lives helps us to remember God's gracious provision and goodness to us.

Day 5:   If standing at the foot of the cross does not cause us to overflow with thankfulness and joy, then we have not stood there long enough.

LORRAINE HILL

Day 1: The Jewel of Joy

> Give thanks in all circumstances, for this is God's will for you
> in Christ Jesus.
>
> 1 Thessalonians 5:18

It's hard to believe that our time has now come to an end. It has
been an exciting but challenging journey, hasn't it? Hopefully you
now have a greater understanding of how to live a joy-filled life
and how not to succumb to the joy stealers. We will end our study
with a week on thankfulness, for thankfulness is the jewel of joy.
Thankfulness increases our level of joy, while unthankfulness tends
to diminish it. Why? Because as we reflect on God's goodness and
express our gratitude more, joy naturally overflows from our hearts.

Read Luke 17:11-19 and answer the following questions.

Who approaches Jesus and for what do they ask?

_____

How many lepers are healed? _____

How many lepers give thanks? _____

Why do you think all of the lepers did not return to give thanks?

_____

In Luke 17:11-19, Jesus is on the way to Jerusalem, traveling along
the border between Samaria and Galilee. Beside the road, ten lepers
call to him, pleading for his help. Because leprosy was contagious,
lepers were required to live outside the city limits, usually in colo-
nies (Leviticus 13:45-46). When Jesus sees the lepers, he makes a
bold statement. He tells them to go and show themselves to the
priests. Jesus's command requires the lepers to step out on faith, for

a leper can only show himself to a priest *after* he has been healed. A priest would inspect the leper and proclaim restoration of health. The leper would then be allowed back into society. All ten lepers follow Jesus's command, and all ten are healed.

Though all ten lepers are healed, only one returns to give thanks to Jesus and to praise him. Jesus, of course, asks the obvious question. Where are the remaining nine lepers? Imagine, only one out of the ten lepers returns to thank Jesus...10 percent. This is not some small act Jesus has performed for these ten men—he has completely cleansed the lepers from their disease. No longer will they stand outside the city gates apart from society, no longer will they feel lonely and isolated from family, no longer will they have inadequate food and drink. This is a life-altering experience for them, and yet only one takes the time to return and thank Jesus. It is interesting, too, that of all the lepers, it is a Samaritan, rather than a Jew, who returns to thank Jesus. The Jews, even more than the Samaritans, know of the importance of praising and thanking God. I wonder, are we sometimes like these nine lepers, exhibiting enough faith in our Christian walk to call out to God yet forgetting the basics of thanksgiving and praise?

What do you learn about the seriousness of ingratitude from Romans 1:21? Why do you think that ingratitude and unthankfulness are such a serious sin?

_____

Have you ever had to lose a blessing in order to realize its value and become thankful for it? Explain.

_____

Fill in the blanks - 1 Thessalonians 5:18.
_____ in _____ circumstances, for this is _____ for you in Christ Jesus.

As we read the story of the ten lepers, we may be a bit surprised by their lack of thankfulness. That is partly because it is much easier to see ingratitude in someone else than in ourselves. So before we throw the first stone, let's examine our own lives. How often do we display unthankful attitudes to the LORD? How often do we take for granted his gracious provision to us? Most of us would acknowledge that we are not by nature thankful creatures. We tend to be far freer with our criticism than our encouragement. For example, if we do not receive appropriate service, we will frequently take time to let our service providers know. But how many times do we write thank you letters for a job well done? In the last year, how many thank you letters have we mailed to our service providers, like our garbage men, hair dressers, grocery store clerks, dry cleaners. Sometimes, this lack of thankfulness transfers to our spiritual lives and to spiritual things. Take our quiet times, for example. Is most of our time centered on thanksgiving or on prayer requests? Sometimes we become so consumed with expressing today's concerns to God that we forget to thank him for fulfilling yesterday's needs. Yet, as many needs as we possess so many needs has God already graciously met for us. Both prayer and thanksgiving are equally important in our relationship with the LORD.

Though unthankfulness characterizes the unredeemed, it should not characterize the children of God. Knowing God should result in our thanksgiving and praise. In fact, one of the great evidences of a Christian's new nature is a thankful and contented spirit. Praise and thanksgiving have always been the response of God's people to God's goodness. The psalms are filled with verses praising God for his goodness. Even the Old Testament Mosaic system included a thanks offering, in which individuals could express gratitude toward the Lord (Leviticus 7:11-15).

In his book *Table Talk*, Martin Luther writes, "The greater God's gifts and works, the less they are regarded."[1] In essence, Martin Luther is saying that the more we receive, the less we are thankful. For example, a child who has only one or two toys is far more appreciative of a new toy than a child whose room and closet overflow with toys. Take a few moments and reflect on this statement. As you have received more from the LORD, have you exhibited a greater degree of thankfulness, or have you instead become casual to God's blessings? Many of us have received great privileges, but instead of producing greater thankfulness in us, it has sometimes generated criticalness and fault-finding. For example, consider the following situations:

- Rather than remaining thankful for the restaurants in which we dine, we may become irritated at the slowness of service.

- Rather than being thankful for grocery stores, we may complain about how long the checkout lines are.

- Rather than rejoicing in our fifteen hundred square foot homes, we may covet our neighbors' twenty-five hundred-square foot homes.

Though we have received great blessings, sometimes we complain about them. Do we consider what an affront to God's gracious provision this is? It is easy to cast stones at the nine lepers, but are we sometimes just as guilty in the eyes of God? To whom much has been given, much is expected. To whom much has been graciously bestowed upon, much thanksgiving is expected.

First Thessalonians 5:18 reminds us that we are to give thanks in all circumstances, not some circumstances, not a few circumstances, but in all circumstances. There are no exceptions. If circumstances are going well, we give thanks because the time of refreshment is a gift of God. If instead we are experiencing a trial, we give thanks because we know that God is working out all things for our good, and our faith is being refined. Notice too that we should give thanks *in* our circumstances, not *after* our circumstances, for it requires little faith to thank God after we see his working.

What does Ephesians 5:18-20 tell us?

_____

Take a few moments and reflect on the following questions (be honest):

What keeps you from overflowing with thanksgiving?

_____

Do you believe that you have a right to certain things?

_____

Do unrealistic expectations help or hinder our thankfulness?

_____

So what hinders our thankfulness? There are many different things, and we will discuss some today and some in the following days.

1.   *Being lukewarm tends to hinder thankfulness.*
As spiritual malaise sets in, we become less grateful for God's blessings. Thankfulness is a thermometer in our lives, revealing our spiritual temperature. On days we allow the Holy Spirit to control us, we tend to express thanks and praise. On days in which we allow our carnal nature to rule us, we tend to complain and criticize.

2.   *A sense of entitlement can impede thankfulness.*
Deep down, we may feel that we deserve better or are entitled to certain privileges. Fundamental to thankfulness is an understanding that life and possessions are not a right but a gracious gift from our Father. If we do not understand that God has graciously given us things, we will develop attitudes of expectancy and create unrealistic expectations. On the other hand, when we begin to better understand that life is a gift and not a right, we will express greater gratitude toward our LORD.

Reclaiming Your Joy

Day 2: Crippled by Complaining

Do everything without complaining or arguing.

Philippians 2:14

Yesterday we started to discuss some of the things that hinder our thankfulness, like being spiritually lukewarm or having a sense of entitlement. Today, we will explore other areas that tend to affect our thankfulness.

Are you a more negative or positive person?
  ☐ Positive   ☐ Negative

Why is a positive attitude important to thankfulness?

_____

3.   *A negative attitude can impede thankfulness.*
Some of you may be like me and tend to be naturally negative people. We see the glass half empty instead of half full. We see the thorns instead of the roses. But if we constantly dwell on the negative, it is hard to appreciate the positive and express thanks for God's blessings. Let me share a story with you to further illustrate this point.

> Jim Smith went to church on Sunday morning. He heard the organist miss a note during the prelude, and he winced. He saw a teenager talking when everybody was supposed to "bow in prayer." He felt like the usher was watching to see what he put in the offering plate, and it made him boil. He caught the preacher making a slip of the tongue five times in the sermon by actual count. As he slipped out through the side door during the closing hymn, he muttered to himself, "Never again! What a bunch of clods and hypocrites!"

LORRAINE HILL

Ron Jones went to church on Sunday morning. He heard the organist play an arrangement of "A Mighty Fortress," and he was thrilled by the majesty of it. He heard a young girl take a moment in the service to speak her simple moving message of the difference her faith makes in her life. He was glad to see that his church was sharing in a special offering for the hungry children of Nigeria. He especially appreciated the sermon that Sunday—it answered a question that had bothered him for a long time. He thought, as he walked out the doors of the church, "How can a man come here and not feel the presence of God?"

Both men went to the same church on the same Sunday morning. Each found what he was looking for.[2]

It's all about perspective, isn't it? And our perspectives are reflections of our hearts. Are they focused outward and upward to receive the majestic revelation of God or focused inward and downward, closing out God's revelation? Some of us have become so focused on the negatives that we are missing all of God's beautiful blessings to us.

4.   *A critical spirit can hinder thankfulness.*

A critical spirit, a spirit that never finds rest in God's abundant provision, strips us bare of the enjoyment of God and the many blessings he richly bestows on us. For the rest of today, we will study about a complaining and critical spirit through the eyes of the Israelites and their journey to freedom. For four hundred years, the Egyptians had enslaved the Israelites. The enslavement was harsh and oppressive so the Israelites call out to the LORD, who sends Moses to deliver them. He leads them through the Red Sea and into the wilderness. Soon after entering the wilderness, the Israelites start to murmur and complain.

Fill out the chart below which describes how the Israelites complain against the LORD.

Israelites' Complaint			God's Response
Exodus 15: 22–24	_____	_____	Exodus 15: 25–26
Exodus 16: 1–3	_____	_____	Exodus 16: 4–8
Numbers 11: 1–3	_____	_____	Numbers 11: 1–3
Numbers 11: 4–6	_____	_____	Numbers 11: 18–20
			Numbers 11: 33–34

As the people grumble to Moses and Aaron, against whom are they really grumbling (Exodus 16:8b)?
☐ Moses and Aaron   ☐ Fellow Israelites   ☐ God

What warning does 1 Corinthians 10:9-11 provide about complaining and grumbling? Do you view your complaining so seriously?

_____

After God delivers the Israelites from the Egyptians, they are infamous for complaining and murmuring. Despite the fact that they have witnessed God's magnificent deeds and his great provision, it takes only three short days before they start murmuring against him. First, they grumble because they lack water. Then, it is manna. Finally, it is quail.

One would think that after receiving the water, manna, and quail, they would have remained more content and trusting, but alas, their critical spirits cannot be assuaged. Do you notice a pattern? Nothing is ever good enough for them—they always seem to want more. Rather than focusing on the LORD's gracious provision and the amazing feats he has shown them, they focus on their wants and their perceived inequities. Does that sound familiar? Sometimes no matter how gracious the Lord's provision, we are never quite satisfied.

God views our complaining attitudes quite seriously. Grumbling is not some small sin that he casually condones. He judges it gravely because it is such an affront to his generosity. In dealing with the Israelites, God sends serpents to bite the complainers, plagues to destroy the grumblers, and fire to consume the outskirts of the camp. Take a moment to allow the magnitude of this to set in. God does not just give his people a sweet warning to stop complaining and grumbling; he kills some of them. Do we honestly view our grumbling in such a serious light? If we do not start to view our complaining as a serious sin, we will not stop doing it. Who are we to argue and complain against our maker? "Woe to him who quarrels with his Maker, to him who is but a potsherd among the potsherds on the ground. Does the clay say to the potter, 'What are you making?' Does your work say, 'he has no hands'?" (Isaiah 45:9).

As the Israelites complain against the Lord, they seem to exercise selective memories. They glamorize their years in Egypt, remembering the fish and the cucumbers and forgetting the slavery and oppression. Instead of celebrating their deliverance, they beg to return to a life of bondage. Can you imagine that they ask to return to a place of slavery and oppression? And what about us? We too can glamorize our pasts, our comforts, and the happiness that we once had. We forget all the difficulties that consumed our previous life and cry out to God for a return to the "happier days." Let's not be like the Israelites—let's not waste countless moments, days, and years exhibiting complaining spirits. In the end, all of our complaining and murmuring does nothing but strip us of the joy of our Christian walk.

Fill in the blanks - Philippians 2:14.

Do _____ things without _____ or _____.

Why should we not complain or grumble (Philippians 2:15)?

What are some creative ways in which Christians can curb their complaining?

Philippians 2:14 commands us to do all things without grumbling or disputing. All things means all things, not some things, not a few things, not when we feel like it, but all things. In his commentary on Philippians, John MacArthur further elaborates on the words grumbling and disputing.

> It [grumbling] is a negative response to something unpleasant, inconvenient, or disappointing, arising from the self-centered notion that it is undeserved...Disputing is from *dialogismos*, which has the basic meaning of inner reasoning and is the term from which the English word *dialogue* derives. But it soon developed the more specific ideas of questioning, doubting, or disputing the truth of a matter.[3]

When we grumble or dispute with God, we show ingratitude for his provision. Have you also noticed how complaining seems to incite additional complaining. It adds fuel to the fire, stirring those around us and giving them license to voice their discontentment.

Before we start to complain or criticize, we need to diligently pray for a situation. We may even need to fast over it. Though it sounds radical given our current society, let me strongly encourage you to start praying and fasting over these situations. This enables us to understand whether our criticism is justified and beneficial or the result of our own selfishness and pettiness. Too often we defend our criticalness based on our desire to help others. But if we are truly trying to help others, then surely spending time on our knees or time fasting for them demonstrates such love. Let's choose to pray instead of criticize, fast instead of complain.

Grumbling and complaining also affects our Christian witness. Philippians 2:15 reminds us that we are to shine like stars in the universe. We do not display much light or beauty when we complain and grumble. We have been placed in a dark world, so let us shine. Let us show the world the magnificence of the LORD we love so much.

Day 3: Praising God's Goodness

> The LORD has done great things for us, and we are filled with joy.
> Psalm 126:3

At the heart of thankfulness is an appreciation of God's goodness to us. We see his goodness reflected in his creation of us, his provision of our daily needs, and his redemption of us. Let's look at each of these areas a little more closely.

What does Genesis 1:1 reveal about God and creation?

_____

According to Revelation 4:11, who created all things?
    ☐ God   ☐ The angels   ☐ A cosmic force

Read Colossians 1:16. For whom was all of creation made?

_____

Genesis 1:1 informs us that God created the heavens and the earth. The Hebrew word used for *God* is *Elohim* and denotes his strength and power. In fact, *El* in Hebrew actually means mighty or strong.

So from the beginning pages of Scripture, we are introduced to our all powerful and mighty God.

In Genesis 1, the Hebrew word *bara* means *created* and is used exclusively of God. It means to create something from nothing. Only God can take nothing and create something beautiful from it. God is *Elohim*, the creator, and he brings everything into existence. Without God, nothing would exist. The universe would not exist. The sun would not exist. The earth would not exist. The oceans would not exist. The land masses would not exist. And we would not exist. As we reflect on the LORD's goodness in creation, it should fill us with great joy and happiness. "The LORD has done great things for us, and we are filled with joy" (Psalm 126:3).

Read Acts 17:24-28. What do you learn about God from Paul's statement?

_____

Why did God make us (Ephesians 1:5)?

_____

Based on the above Scriptures, did God have to make us?
☐ Yes   ☐ No

How does knowing that God did not have to make you but chose to do so help you feel more joyful and thankful? Reflect on Psalm 92:4.

_____

Though God's creation alone should cause us to stand in awe of him, our reverence goes even deeper when we realize that God did not have to make us. Ephesians 1:5 says that God created us for his good will and pleasure. God did not make us to fill a need he had, for God has no needs. He is *El Shaddai*, the self-sufficient or all sufficient one. God is self-existent and thus does not depend on anyone or anything for his existence (Exodus 3:14). All that God needs is perfectly contained within himself. From all of eternity, God the Father, God the Son, and God the Holy Spirit have enjoyed perfect fellowship and communion. In his book on *Systematic Theology*, Wayne Grudem further elaborates, "In fact, the love and interpersonal fellowship, and the sharing of glory, have always been and will always be far more perfect than any communion we as finite human beings will ever have with God."[4] This takes a moment to absorb, doesn't it? Sometimes we feel the world revolves around us and our wants, and yet God never had to make us. He chose to make us for his good will and pleasure.

This may lead us to believe that we are insignificant or unimportant, but that is not true either. Wayne Grudem encouragingly points out, "to be significant to God is to be significant in the most ultimate sense. No greater personal significance can be imagined."[5] I must also stress that just because God never had to make us does not mean that he does not love us tremendously or derive great pleasure from us—he does, and we bring him great joy!

God also graciously continues to provide for us and for all of his creation. He is not too busy for any of us. "The eyes of all look to you, and you give them their food at the proper time. You open your hand and satisfy the desires of every living thing" (Psalm 145:15-16). As we reflect on God's creation and care of us, we should be enjoined to passionately praise our LORD and to joyously proclaim his goodness to others. There is joy from daily grace and from knowing that God walks with us everyday.

> Sing to the LORD a new song; sing to the LORD, all the earth.
> Sing to the LORD, praise his name; proclaim his salvation day after day. Declare his glory among the nations, his marvelous deeds among all peoples.
>
> Psalm 96:1-3

Sometimes, it is not that we mean to be unthankful but rather that we become accustomed to God's goodness and provision. We become so comfortable in God's blessings that we forget to take time to thank him.

What are some creative ways that can enable us to remain more thankful and appreciative of God's blessings?

_____

_____

Here are a few creative suggestions for how we can remain more thankful:

- Start our quiet time by thanking God for at least ten bless-ings. This creates a thankful mood as we enter the LORD's presence. It also allows the LORD to open our eyes to his amazing provision. Let's be creative and list new blessings each day.

- Keep a thankfulness journal in which we record different things for which we are thankful. Over the years, we will enjoy reviewing some of our past thanks.

- Create a thankfulness jar for the whole family. Discuss everyone's thankfulness at dinner or during some spe-cially appointed time. This helps pass down a thankfulness legacy to our children so that they better understand that blessings are a gift from God and not their entitlement.

- Go outside and take a praise walk. Take a few moments to relax and enjoy God's beautiful world and to praise him for it.

- Have a Thankful Thursday or any other day in which we serve the underprivileged. Focusing on others who pos-sess less than us enables us to better appreciate God's great blessings to us.

- Fast for a day. Nothing helps us to appreciate food and God's gracious provision better than going without food for a day. We will find ourselves spiritually refreshed and renewed.

- Learn to count our blessings. Someone has said that we should never count our troubles until we have counted at least one hundred of our blessings. By then, we will have forgotten our troubles and what we think we lack. Remember Johnson Oatman Jr.'s song "Count Your Blessings."

Count your blessings, name them one by one,
Count your blessings, see what God hath done!

Exercise

As we end today, take a few moments to list nine blessings that the LORD has given you. If you cannot think of nine, then pause and allow the Holy Spirit to help you.

1. _____ 2. _____ 3. _____

4. _____ 5. _____ 6. _____

7. _____ 8. _____ 9. _____

Day 4: Making Memorials

Praise the LORD, O my soul, and forget not all his benefits.

Psalm 103:2

Yesterday we started discussing some creative ways that help us focus on the LORD's goodness and provision to us. A final way is to create memorials in our lives. Memorials are reminders of significant events and people, both good and bad. They remind us of struggles and victories, losses and blessings.

Read Joshua 3 and answer the following questions.

What is Israel about to do? _____

Who is Israel's current leader?   ☐ Moses   ☐ Joshua

Why is crossing the Jordan River miraculous? _____

Challenge

What similarities and differences do you notice between Israel crossing the Jordan River and her crossing the Red Sea (compare Joshua 3 with Exodus 14)?

Similarities: _____

Differences: _____

As Joshua 3 opens, the whole nation of Israel is poised to enter the promised land. First, however, they have to cross the Jordan River, which is at flood stage due to the harvest season. So God provides for his people by performing a miracle. As soon as the priests carrying the Ark of the Covenant set foot on the Jordan River, its waters dry up. The Ark of the Covenant represents God's presence in his people; thus the priests carry it first. Due to the ark's sacredness, the people follow at a distance. Because God miraculously causes the waters of the Jordan River to dry up, the whole nation enters the promised land. Imagine, thousands of people cross, and not one is lost, and they cross on dry, hard ground (Joshua 3:17).

Why does God perform such a miracle for Israel? God's miraculous provision serves many purposes: first, it enables the Israelites to cross into their promised land. Second, it confirms that God will be with Joshua as he has been with Moses (Joshua 3:7). Joshua will serve as the new leader for the people. And third, it provides encouragement to the people as they start to conquer their promised land (Joshua 3:9-11).

Read Joshua 4 about Israel's crossing into the promised land and answer the following questions.

What does the LORD instruct the Israelites to do? _____

How many stones are used?   ☐ 12   ☐ 15

What do the stones represent? _____

Why do the Israelites need to build a memorial? _____

What warning had God given the Israelites in Deuteronomy 8:10-14?

_____

Read Psalm 103:1-5 and fill in the blank.
Praise the LORD, O my soul, and _____ not all his benefits

Challenge
The LORD instituted several feasts to help the Israelites remember his deeds and goodness. What do the feasts represent? Match the feast with its corresponding description.

_____ Feast of Weeks (Leviticus 23:15-21)
_____ Passover (Exodus 12:1-14)
_____ First fruits (Leviticus 23:9-14)
_____ Sabbath (Exodus 20:8-11)
_____ Feast of Trumpets (Leviticus 23:23-25)
_____ Day of Atonement (Leviticus 23:26-32)
_____ Feast of Tabernacles (Leviticus 23:33-43)

A) Atone for the sins of the priests and people
B) Remember journey from Egypt to Canaan
C) Rest from labor on the seventh day
D) Thankfulness for the harvest
E) Gratitude for the LORD's bounty in the land
F) Day of rest commemorated with trumpets
G) Remember deliverance from Egypt

Why do you think it is important to not forget what the LORD has done for us? Also see Job 8:12-13.

Before conquering the promised land, the LORD instructs the Israelites to create a memorial at Gilgal. The memorial will consist of twelve stones, representing the twelve tribes of Israel and will serve as a continual sign among the people of God's provision. In the future, the Israelites will tell their children that the LORD stopped the flow of the Jordan River to allow the Israelites to cross. The LORD repeatedly told the Israelites to not forget his acts of goodness. The Hebrew word for *forget*

> indicates that something has been lost to memory, or a period of time has softened the memory of it...It is an especially important word with respect to God and his people: God never forgets them (Isaiah 49:15); they are not to forget their God, his covenant, and his deeds.[6]

During times of ease and comfort, there is a tendency to become proud and self-sufficient and to forget the LORD's blessings. Abundance has the ability to lull one into forgetfulness. And forgetfulness often leads to disobedience, pride, idolatry, and a whole host of other sins. Thus, the LORD warns the Israelites and us to not forget him or to become softened to the memory of his great deeds. The memorial also enables pagan nations to glimpse the greatness of God.

The Jordan River memorial is the first of a series of memorials that the Israelites will establish to remember God: others include the ruins of Jericho (Joshua 6:26), Achan's body (Joshua 7:26), the King of Ai (Joshua 8:29), and Mount Ebal (Joshua 8:30-31). God also institutes other reminders to the Israelites—feasts, thanks offerings, altars, and even tassels (Numbers 15:37-41).

Just like the Israelites had memorials, so we too also have memorials in our lives. What are some of these memorials?

- *Baptism*: After accepting Jesus as our LORD and Savior, many of us were baptized. This day of celebration symbolizes our new birth in Christ.

- *The Lord's Supper (Communion)*: Every time we participate in the LORD's Supper, we remember Christ's redemption of us. This is a time when we celebrate God's grace and sacrifice for us. Most of us celebrate our physical birthdays, but how exciting to also celebrate our spiritual birthdays!

- *Trials*: Our trials can also serve as Memorials in our Christian walk, special times of fellowship with our LORD. Let's make sure that we remember these times, perhaps by journaling them, so that we can see how the LORD has worked in our lives.

- *Victories*: We need to celebrate our victories. Perhaps we have been through an exceedingly difficult season. Let's praise God and thank him for seeing us through it. We could commemorate our victories by composing poems or writing praise songs. For instance, when Hannah finally conceived, after years and years of prayer, she composed a song to the LORD (1 Samuel 2). We need to take time to ponder how God has enabled us to experience our great victories. "I will remember the deeds of the LORD; yes, I will remember your miracles of long ago. I will meditate on all your works and consider all your mighty deeds" (Psalm 77:11-12).

- *Failings*: Even our failings can serve as memorials in our Christian walk. Sometimes the LORD allows us to remember those times we have failed him (though we have been completely forgiven) to keep us from returning to those dark and miserable places.

Exercise

Describe some of the different memorials in your life and what they mean to you.

Day 5: The Garment of Salvation

I delight greatly in the LORD; my soul rejoices in my God. For he has clothed me with garments of salvation and arrayed me in a robe of righteousness.

Isaiah 61:10a

For the past few days we have been discussing how God's goodness is manifested in our lives. There is no greater manifestation of God's goodness and mercy than our salvation, so we will devote the rest of today to remembering the greatness of our salvation.

As redeemed children of God, we have been saved from hell. How is this place described in Matthew 8:12 and Jude 1:7b?

_____

Read Isaiah 61:10. Now that we are saved, in what has God clothed us?

 With _____ and a _____

What should be our response to our salvation?

Psalm 35:9 _____

Hebrews 12:28 _____

Read Luke 10:17-20 and fill in the blank.
Do not to rejoice that the spirits submit to you, but rejoice that
_____ (Luke 10:20).

How many times in the last week did you thank God for your salvation? Do you tend to take your salvation for granted?
☐ 0-5   ☐ 6-10   ☐ 11+

Joy and thankfulness should bubble forth from our mouths as we reflect on the greatness of our redemption. There is no greater gift that God could give us than the gift of salvation - we have been saved from hell, given eternity with God, restored to a wondrous relationship with the LORD, have experienced the daily forgiveness of sins, and have received a great inheritance. Let's take a moment and really reflect on this.

- First and foremost, we have been saved from hell, a place of eternal torment and suffering. Scripture describes hell as a lake of fire, burning sulfur, and a fiery furnace. There will be "weeping and gnashing of teeth" and darkness (Matthew 13:42). Hell is the final place for sinners who do not accept Christ, and it represents complete isolation from the righteous. No matter what we envision hell to be, the reality will be far worse. Yet we have been saved from this.

- But our blessings do not end here. We have been given the wondrous privilege of a relationship with God. We can now spend eternity with God, learning more about him and enjoying his presence. Could we ever ask for more?

- And yet God does provide even more. He also gives us an inheritance. God has poured out and is currently pouring out one blessing after another on us. Romans 8:17 tells us that we are co-heirs with Christ.

Even if we receive nothing this world offers, we still have everything! And if we truly believe this, then joy should resound from our souls every minute of every day. In Luke 10:20, Jesus told the disciples not to rejoice that the spirits submitted to them but rather that their names were written in heaven. Even though their service was exciting, it was even more exciting that they were saved. The Greek word for *written*, *eggrapho*, means the "state of completion, stand written, enrolled or engraved."[7] Nothing compares to the fact that our names are engraved in heaven, not even experiencing great victories in our service for the LORD. "Thanks be to God for his indescribable gift!" (2 Corinthians 9:15).

Years ago, during one of my pity-party moments, I was complaining and being very unthankful. I was not feeling well, and circumstances were not going my way. So I indulged myself and wallowed in self-pity to my husband. As always, he patiently listened and then succinctly said, "Lorraine, you have salvation. What more do you want?" Pretty profound, wasn't it? Well, I have to be honest, in that moment I could have listed for you everything else I wanted: for God to restore my health, for him to change my circumstances, for him to give me pleasant co-workers, and so forth. At the moment, I was too immersed in my self-pity to understand the magnitude of what my husband said. But it really is that simple—we have salvation. What more do we want? If we want more, than we have not yet understood the greatness of our salvation. Charles Spurgeon, the famous preacher who lived in the nineteenth century, once said,

> Stand at the foot of the cross, and count the purple drops by which you have been cleansed: See the thorn-crown;

mark his scourged shoulders, still gushing with encrimsoned rills.... And if you do not lie prostrate on the ground before that cross, you have never seen it.[8]

What about us? Have we seen the cross? Have we understood what it cost Jesus to redeem us? Do we understand the greatness of our salvation? Perhaps with all the busyness and stresses of this life, we need to take a moment and reflect on it.

Spend some time reading and really reflecting on the following passages. What new insight did the Holy Spirit bring you about Jesus's redemption of your life?

Isaiah 52:13-53:12 _____

John 19:1-30 _____

Philippians 2:5-8 _____

Take a few moments to reflect on how your salvation has changed your life. How can reflecting on your salvation enable you to remain more thankful and joyous?

_____

If you are like me, over time you have the tendency to take your salvation for granted and to become casual to it. We forget what it took for Jesus to redeem us. So let's spend a few *very brief* moments discussing our salvation and its great cost to our LORD.

- Jesus, the transcendent God, who existed through all of eternity, who created this world, who hand-crafted you and me, chooses to take the form of a man. He does not cling to his position in heaven, where legions of angels constantly worship him, but willingly surrenders it. He also does not mind giving up his infinite beauty to be constrained by arms, legs, and a body. And he comes, not as a powerful king, but as a baby born in a lowly stable.

- While on earth, Jesus lives in the simplest of places, having only a basic home. He does not enjoy many of the conveniences that we enjoy today, like air conditioning, modern transportation, and running water. Imagine, Jesus has unlimited benefits and blessings in heaven and yet chooses to leave them for us.

- Much of Jesus's life is spent being misunderstood and mocked. He endures taunts, false accusations, and public shame. He is rejected and hated by many of his own people. One of his closest friends, Judas, even betrays him.

- And then the time comes for him to lay down his life for us, to become the atoning sacrifice for our sins. In the garden of Gethsemane, as Jesus prays God's will, his emotional suffering is so intense that he actually sweats blood.

- Jesus's means of death, crucifixion, is so lowly that the Romans reserved it for the worst of criminals. It is one of the cruelest forms of death, involving excruciating pain and intense suffering. A prisoner was flogged, beaten, and then forced to carry his own cross.

- Though it is agonizingly painful, Jesus endures. His physical abuse is followed by verbal taunts and ridicule. Pilate, the Roman officials, the guards, the crowds all taunt and mock him. He could have stopped it at any moment; he could have chosen to go back to the Father; he could have used his powers. Legions of angels stood at his disposal, but he doesn't—he chooses to endure for you and for me.

- The time finally arrives for his crucifixion. The soldiers take Jesus to crucify him, but Jesus is so weakened from his flogging that he cannot even carry his cross; so Simon of Cyrene, a passer-by, carries Jesus's cross for him. Jesus, our beloved Savior, is crucified, like a common criminal, between two thieves. This is the death our Savior chooses not because he is a sinner but because you and I are. The just dying for the unjust, the sinless for the sinful.

- From noon until about 3 PM, an eerie darkness covers the city. Then Jesus cries out, " 'Eloi, Eloi, lama sabachthani?' which means, 'My God, my God, why have you forsaken me?' " (Matthew 27:46). Having always known beautiful fellowship with the Father, Jesus now experiences spiritual separation as he feels the sins of the world heaped upon him. And all the while, we are his vile enemies, cursing, spitting, and mocking him.

- Then Jesus utters those sweet and beautiful words, "It is finished" (John 19:30). It is done. Redemption has been secured for us. But let us never think that it is not costly. Our redemption cost Jesus an agonizingly painful death. It cost God the Father his beloved and precious Son. And it cost the Holy Spirit centuries of dealing with the sinful, hardened hearts of men.[9]

This is the death our beloved Savior chose so that we could be reconciled to the Father and spend eternity in his wondrous presence. Have we now seen the cross? Though salvation cost us nothing, it cost our LORD much. We must place things in perspective. God did not have to redeem us. Yet Jesus, knowing that his road would be marked with intense pain and suffering, chose to redeem us anyway. As we reflect on the greatness of our salvation, joy should overflow from our lips and into our lives. We should be unable to stop the overwhelming gratitude that we feel. If standing at Calvary has not created thankfulness and joy in us, then we have not stood there long enough. "But may all who seek you rejoice and be glad in you; may those who love your salvation always say, 'The LORD be exalted!' " (Psalms 40:16).

Endnotes

Week 1: Our Great Calling

1. C. S. Lewis, *Letters to Malcolm: Chiefly on Prayer* (New York: Harcourt, Brace & World, 1963), 93.

2. Archibald Thomas Robertson, *Word Pictures in the New Testament: Volume VI - The General Epistles and the Revelation of John* (Grand Rapids, MI: Baker Book House, 1933), 84.

3. Spiros Zodhiates ThD., gen. ed., *The Complete Word Study Dictionary New Testament*, (Chattanooga, TN: AMG Publishers, 1992), #5479, 1467.

4. C. S. Lewis, *Mere Christianity and the Screwtape Letters* (New York: HarperSanFrancisco, 2003), 134.

5. Archibald Thomas Robertson, *Word Pictures in the New Testament: Volume IV - The Epistles of Paul*, Volume IV (Grand Rapids, MI: Baker Book House, 1931), 505.

6. C. S. Lewis, *The Weight of Glory* (New York: HarperSanFrancisco, 1949), 26.

7. Zodhiates, *The Complete Word Study Dictionary New Testament*, #4657, 1298.

Week 2: Abiding Joy

1. Spiros Zodhiates Th.D., gen. ed., *The Complete Word Study Dictionary New Testament*, (Chattanooga, TN: AMG Publishers, 1992), #1401, 483.

2. John MacArthur Jr., *Galatians* (Chicago, IL: Moody Press, 1987), 13.

3. Zodhiates, *The Complete Word Study Dictionary New Testament*, #926, 324.

4. Warren W. Wiersbe, *Be Free* (Wheaton, IL: Victor Books, 1984), 116.

5. Archibald Thomas Robertson, *Word Pictures in the New Testament: Volume VI - The General Epistles and the Revelation of John* (Grand Rapids, MI: Baker Book House, 1933), 18.

Week 3: Weighed Down by Worry

1. Warren W. Wiersbe, *Be Loyal* (Colorado Springs, CO: Victor Publishing, 2004), 47.

2. Warren Baker D.R.E. and Eugene Carpenter Ph.D., *The Complete Word Study Dictionary Old Testament* (Chattanooga, TN: AMG Publishers, 2003), #1556, 204.

3. John MacArthur Jr., *Philippians* (Chicago, IL: Moody Press, 2001), 284.

4. Elizabeth Barrett Browning, *Aurora Leigh and Other Poems* (New York, NY: Penguin Books, 1995), 232.

Week 4: Wearied by People

1. Spiros Zodhiates ThD., gen. ed., *The Complete Word Study Dictionary New Testament,* Chattanooga, TN: AMG Publishers, 1992), #3948, 1122.

2. Ibid., #4355, 1235.

3. Frederick C. Mish, ed., "Meaning of Compassion," *Merriam-Webster's Collegiate Dictionary,* eleventh ed., (Springfield, MA: Merriam-Webster, Incorporated, 2003), 253.

4. Archibald Thomas Robertson, *Word Pictures in the New Testament: Volume I - The Gospel According to Matthew, The Gospel According to Mark* (Grand Rapids, MI: Baker Book House, 1930), 116.

5. Zodhiates, *The Complete Word Study Dictionary New Testament,* #700, 251.

6. Warren Baker D.R.E., Eugene Carpenter Ph.D., *The Complete Word Study Dictionary Old Testament (*Chattanooga, TN: AMG Publishers, 2003), #4170, 585.

Week 5: Downcast by Disappointment

1. Warren W. Wiersbe, *Be Skillful* (Colorado Springs, CO: ChariotVictor Publishing, 1995), 38.

2. J. Oswald Sanders, *Spiritual Manpower (Formerly titled Robust in Faith)* (Chicago, IL: Moody Press, 1965), 44.

3. Charles R. Swindoll, *Joseph - A Man of Absolute Integrity* (Nashville, TN: Word Publishing, 1998), 65.

4. Gene A. Getz, *Joseph: Overcoming Obstacles Through Faithfulness* (Nashville, TN: Broadman & Holman, 1996). 108.

5. Ibid., 94.

6. Ibid.

7. Warren Baker D.R.E., Eugene Carpenter Ph.D., *The Complete Word Study Dictionary Old Testament* (Chattanooga, TN: AMG Publishers, 2003), #7797, 1117.

8. Warren W. Wiersbe, *Be Satisfied* (Wheaton, IL: Victor Books, 1990), 87.

Week 6: Imprisoned by Unforgiveness

1. C. S. Lewis, *Mere Christianity and the Screwtape Letters* (New York: HarperSanFrancisco, 2003), 115.

2. Spiros Zodhiates Th.D., gen. ed., *The Complete Word Study Dictionary New Testament,* (Chattanooga, TN: AMG Publishers, 1992), #3049, 922.

3. Warren W. Wiersbe, *Be Loyal* (Colorado Springs, CO: Victor Publishing, 2004), 130.

4. C. S. Lewis, *The Inspirational Writing of C. S. Lewis* (New York: Inspirational Press, 1991), 328.

5. John MacArthur, Jr. *The Freedom and Power of Forgiveness* (Wheaton, IL: Crossway Books, 1998), 85.

6. Zodhiates, *The Complete Word Study Dictionary New Testament,* #5136, 1393.

7. Corrie Ten Boom and Jamie Buckingham, *Tramp for the Lord* (Fort Washington, PA: Christian Literature Crusade and Fleming H. Revell Company, 1974), 56-57.

Week 7: Troubled by Trials

1. Spiros Zodhiates ThD., gen. ed., *The Complete Word Study Dictionary New Testament*, (Chattanooga, TN: AMG Publishers, 1992), #5483, 1468.

2. Charles Spurgeon quoted in Warren W. Wiersbe, *Be Daring* (Colorado Springs, CO: ChariotVictor Publishing, 1988), 40.

3. Zodhiates, *The Complete Word Study Dictionary New Testament*, #21, 64.

4. Oswald Chambers, *My Utmost for His Highest* (Uhrichsville, OH: Barbour Publishing, 1963), April 19.

5. Zodhiates, *The Complete Word Study Dictionary New Testament*, #1689, 573.

6. Clive Staples Lewis, *The Complete C. S. Lewis Signature Classics* (New York: HarperCollins, 2002), 604.

7. Elizabeth J. Jewell and Frank Abate, *The New Oxford American Dictionary*, 2nd edition (New York, NY: Oxford University Press, 2005), 1713.

Week 8: Abounding in Thankfulness

1. R. J. Morgan, *Nelson's Complete Book of Stories, Illustrations, and Quotes* (Nashville, TN: Thomas Nelson Publishers, 2000), electronic edition.

2. Ibid.

3. John MacArthur Jr., *Philippians* (Chicago, IL: Moody Press, 2001), 179-180.

4. Wayne Grudem, *Systematic Theology* (Grand Rapids, MI: Zondervan, 1994), 161.

5. Ibid., 163.

6. Warren Baker D.R.E. and Eugene Carpenter Ph.D., *The Complete Word Study Dictionary Old Testament* (Chattanooga, TN: AMG Publishers, 2003), #7911, 1136.

7. Archibald Thomas Robertson, *Word Pictures in the New Testament: Volume II - The Gospel According to Luke* (Grand Rapids, MI: Baker Book House, 1930), 148-149.

8. Morgan, *Nelson's Complete Book of Stories, Illustrations and Quotes*, electronic edition.

9. Robert Shank, *Life in the Son* (Minneapolis, MN: Bethany, 1989), 14.

LORRAINE HILL

Bibliography

Baker, Warren and Eugene Carpenter. *The Complete Word Study Dictionary Old Testament.* Chattanooga, TN: AMG Publishers, 2003.

Boom, Corrie Ten and Jamie Buckingham. *Tramp for the Lord.* Fort Washington, PA: Christian Literature Crusade and Fleming H. Revell Company, 1974.

Browning, Elizabeth Barrett. *Aurora Leigh and Other Poems.* New York, NY: Penguin Books, 1995.

Chambers, Oswald. *My Utmost for His Highest.* Uhrichsville, OH: Barbour Publishing, 1963.

Getz, Gene A. *Joseph: Overcoming Obstacles Through Faithfulness.* Nashville, TN: Broadman & Holman, 1996.

Grudem, Wayne. *Systematic Theology.* Grand Rapids, MI: Zondervan, 1994.

Jewell, Elizabeth J. and Frank Abate. *The New Oxford American Dictionary.* Second Edition. New York, NY: Oxford University Press, 2005.

Lewis, C. S. *The Complete C. S. Lewis Signature Classics.* New York: HarperCollins, 2002.

Lewis, C. S. *The Inspirational Writing of C. S. Lewis*. New York: Inspirational Press, 1991.

Lewis, C. S. *Letters to Malcolm: Chiefly on Prayer*. New York: Harcourt, Brace & World, 1963.

Lewis, C. S. *Mere Christianity and the Screwtape Letters*. New York: HarperSanFrancisco, 2003.

Lewis, C. S. *The Weight of Glory*. New York: HarperSanFrancisco, 1949.

MacArthur, John Jr. *Galatians*. Chicago, IL: Moody Press, 1987.

MacArthur, John Jr. *Philippians*. Chicago, IL: Moody Press, 2001.

MacArthur, John Jr. *The Freedom and Power of Forgiveness*. Wheaton, IL: Crossway Books, 1998.

Mish, Frederick C., ed. *Merriam-Webster's Collegiate Dictionary*. Eleventh Edition. Springfield, MA: Merriam-Webster, Incorporated, 2003.

Morgan, R. J. *Nelson's Complete Book of Stories, Illustrations, and Quotes*. Nashville, TN: Thomas Nelson Publishers, 2000, Electronic Edition.

Robertson, Archibald Thomas. *Word Pictures in the New Testament: Volume I - The Gospel According to Matthew, The Gospel According to Mark*. Grand Rapids, MI: Baker Book House, 1930.

Robertson, Archibald Thomas. *Word Pictures in the New Testament: Volume II - The Gospel According to Luke*. Grand Rapids, MI: Baker Book House, 1930.

Robertson, Archibald Thomas. *Word Pictures in the New Testament: Volume IV - The Epistles of Paul,* Volume IV. Grand Rapids, MI: Baker Book House, 1931.

Robertson, Archibald Thomas. *Word Pictures in the New Testament: Volume VI - The General Epistles and the Revelation of John.* Grand Rapids, MI: Baker Book House, 1933.

Sanders, J. Oswald. *Spiritual Manpower, formerly titled Robust in Faith.* Chicago, IL: Moody Press, 1965.

Shank, Robert. *Life in the Son.* Minneapolis, MN: Bethany, 1989.

Swindoll, Charles R. *A Man of Absolute Integrity Joseph.* Nashville, TN: Word Publishing, 1998.

Wiersbe, Warren W. *Be Daring.* Colorado Springs, CO: ChariotVictor Publishing, 1988.

Wiersbe, Warren W. *Be Free.* Wheaton, IL: Victor Books, 1984.

Wiersbe, Warren W. *Be Loyal.* Colorado Springs, CO: Victor Publishing, 2004.

Wiersbe, Warren W. *Be Satisfied.* Wheaton, IL: Victor Books, 1990.

Wiersbe, Warren W. *Be Skillful.* Colorado Springs, CO: ChariotVictor Publishing, 1995.

Zodhiates, Spiros. *The Complete Word Study Dictionary New Testament.* Chattanooga, TN: AMG Publishers, 1992.